Series Editor Scott Miles

Effective
Reading

Amanda French

4

Upper Intermediate

MACMILLAN

Macmillan Education
Between Towns Road, Oxford OX4 3PP
A division of Macmillan Publishers Limited
Companies and representatives throughout the world

ISBN 978-0-230-02917-0

First published 2010

Original design by Designers Collective
Page make-up by Marie Prime and Richard Prime; Julian Littlewood
Illustrated by Ed McLachlan
Cover design by Designers Collective
Cover illustration/photograph by Designers Collective

**The authors and publishers would like to thank the following for
permission to use copyright material:**
Extract from 'Speckled Band & Other Stories' retold by Anne Collins for Macmillan
Readers (Macmillan Publishers 2005), copyright © Anne Collins 2005, reprinted by
permission of the publisher;
Extract from 'Dracula' retold by Margaret Tarner for Macmillan Readers
(Macmillan Publishers 2005), copyright © Margaret Tarner 2005, reprinted by
permission of the publisher;
Interview and information about 'Simon Flower the musician' used by permission of
Simon Flower.

These materials may contain links for third-party websites. We have no control
over, and are not responsible for, the contents of such third-party websites. Please
use care when accessing them.

**The authors and publishers would like to thank the following for
permission to reproduce their photographs:**
AFP p116; **Alamy** / Manor Photography p61; **Brand X** p83; **Corbis** / BBNJ
Productions p104, Corbis / Bettmann Archive pp101, 146, Corbis / Fabio Cardoso
p38, Corbis / Comstock p73, Corbis / Najlah Feanny p6, Corbis / Patrick Gianrdino
p50, Corbis / Simon Marcus p132, Corbis / Kazuyoshi Noamachi p58, Corbis /
Reuters p23, Corbis / Veer p82, Corbis / Zefa pp94, 126; **Courtesy of Simon
Flowers** / © Jonathan Pilkington 2007 p123; **Damien Hirst** The Physical
Impossibility of Death in the Mind of Someone Living 1991 Glass, steel, silicon,
formaldehyde solution and shark 2170 x 5420 x 1800 mm Photo: Prudence
Cuming Associates / © Damien Hirst. All rights reserved, DACS 2009 p60; **Design
Pics** p72; **Digital Vision** p28; **John Foxx Images** p105; **Getty** p96; **Imagebank**
p30; **istock** p35; **Panoramic** p16; **Rex Features** / Focus / Everett p40, Rex
Features / Network / Everett p50. **Stone** p106; **Superstock** p7; **Taxi** p67.

Whilst every effort has been made to locate the owners of copyright material in
this book, there may have been some cases when the publishers have been unable
to contact the owners. We should be grateful to hear from anyone who recognises
copyright material and who is unacknowledged. We shall be pleased to make the
necessary amendments in future editions of the book.

Printed in Thailand

2014 2013 2012 2011
10 9 8 7 6 5 4 3 2

'*Choose an author as you choose a friend.*'

Wentworth Dillon, Lord Roscommon *Essay on Translated Verse* 1684

Contents

1 • Language

PRE-READING 1   **Read the subtitle of the text and guess the meaning of** *euphemism*.

A euphemism is ...

a   a word or phrase that means one thing and is used to refer to another thing, in order to emphasize their similar qualities.

b   a phrase or idea that is boring because people use it a lot and it is no longer original.

c   a word or expression that people use when they want to talk about something unpleasant or embarrassing without mentioning the thing itself.

The other two definitions are for *cliché* **and** *metaphor***. Decide which is the correct definition for these words.**

PRE-READING 2   **Which of the following words are usually connected to language (L) and which are usually connected to war (W)? Write L or W. Find the words in bold in the text to help you.**

1   to dumb down   ☐

2   to be inarticulate   ☐

3   to translate   ☐

4   a civilian   ☐

5   a target   ☐

6   a campaign   ☐

The power of double-speak

Euphemisms have been used since ancient times to avoid giving offensc, but now politicians are using them to hide the realities of war.

Deferred success, person who is hearing-impaired – are these phrases in any current dictionary? Where did they originate? Does anyone actually use them? While our media are frequently charged with **dumbing down** and our teenagers with **being inarticulate**, and perhaps both accusations have merit, some of our leaders are busy creating a whole new vocabulary. Listen to political speeches these days and you'll find yourself having to spontaneously **translate** newly-combined words from your own language. It could be the Minister for Education finding reasons why our children are now leaving school without having mastered simple arithmetic (they're motivationally challenged), or someone from the Department of Transportation explaining why the differently-abled are still denied access to numerous subway lines. All politicians seem to be semi-fluent in double-speak.

The ancient Greeks used euphemisms for certain religious words so they did not offend the gods. Native English speakers in previous centuries used euphemisms mainly to avoid giving offence to each other. Better to say 'I have to visit the rest room' than directly announcing your intention to use the toilet. 'He passed away yesterday' is a bit more sensitive than 'Tom has just died'. As we know, language evolves with time and trends. So now we have the rather modern 'She's rather full figured', which is certainly kinder than 'She's fat'! Even more recently, 'blended family' has been used to replace the much longer 'Divorcees Jack and Mary have got married and their kids from previous relationships are now one big family'. But in the 21st century, the use of euphemism or double-speak is also being exploited for far more sinister purposes. If you don't believe this, listen hard to what our military leaders are really telling us and read between the lines of the next 'factual' report on any country afflicted by war.

Even if you deplore their policies, you have to agree that our military leaders are clever. Once you dehumanize the enemy, it's far easier to drop your bombs and mask the horror of war. Your own **civilians** reading the paper or listening to their leaders on the evening news are less likely to protest or comprehend the claim that 'An attack on soft **targets** is the only way to destroy the terrorists hiding among them' than the admission that 'We

also had to kill innocent men, women, and children who lived in the town.' We are now so used to double-speak that we are in danger of becoming truly desensitized. We hear about military **campaigns** and the statistics of death, but the actual gruesome
45 details are quite remote. Our politicians and our generals know that if we actually saw what is left after a bomb has dropped and witnessed the grief of the survivors, we might demand an end to the fighting.

The greatest hypocrisy, of course, is the use of language to glorify
50 or justify the actions of your army and then to denounce exactly the same actions when they are carried out by the opposing army. A military report that announces 'Our soldiers were forced to take cover' is factually no different from the statement that 'Their soldiers ran away and disappeared,' but the latter sounds far more
55 cowardly. And, of course, when the government supports the actions of a rebel group that it believes could serve as a potentially useful ally, the rebels are more likely to be called 'freedom fighters'. This label instantly creates an image of bravery and selflessness. As soon as the government decides that the
60 group might not be a useful ally after all, its members become 'terrorists'; in other words, evil and inhumane. Whether you realize it or not, your opinions are being made for you by the words that someone else chooses to say or write.

When I was child, I used to believe that war was about good versus
65 evil, and it was easy to know whose side you should be on. Now when I hear of another case of young soldiers being killed by 'friendly fire', I almost wish I was still that naïve.

POST READING   **Match the euphemisms to their meanings below. Look for similarities in vocabulary.**

euphemism

1 deferred success   2 hearing impaired   3 motivationally challenged

4 soft target   5 friendly fire

meaning

a shots fired at you accidentally by soldiers from your own army

b the bombing of an area where civilians live

c to be deaf

d to under-perform (at school)

e a failure

COMPREHENSION 1   **Decide if the information about the text is True (T), False (F), or Not Given (NG). Write T, F, or NG.**

1   The quality of newspaper and TV reports is sub-standard.   ☐

2   Politicians are borrowing words from other languages for their speeches.   ☐

3   Native English speakers are less polite than they used to be.   ☐

4   People often fail to understand the use of euphemism in the media.   ☐

5   The use of euphemism has made people indifferent to other people's suffering.   ☐

6   Military leaders do not admit that their soldiers need to hide from the enemy.   ☐

COMPREHENSION 2   **Use the words and phrases in the box to re-write the sentences from the text.**

make	genuine	react	evil	criticize	risk	used
explain	reality	frequently	good	reasons	wrongly
less real and important	care	hide	moral beliefs

1   Euphemism is being exploited for far more sinister purposes.

Euphemism is being (**a**) _____ (**b**) _____ for much more

(**c**) _____ (**d**) _____.

2   Once you dehumanize the enemy, it's far easier to drop your bombs and mask the horror of war.

After you (**a**) _____ your enemies (**b**) _____, it is far easier

to drop bombs on them and (**c**) _____ the (**d**) _____ of war.

3   We are now so used to double-speak that we are in danger of becoming truly desensitized.

Military leaders and politicians use double-speak so (**a**) _____

that there is a (**b**) _____ that people will no longer (**c**) _____

about or (**d**) _____ to the suffering of war victims.

4   The greatest hypocrisy ... is the use of language to ... justify the actions of your army and ... to denounce exactly the same actions when they are carried out by the opposing army.

Your (**a**) _____ are not (**b**) _____ if you use language to

(**c**) _____ why the actions of your army are (**d**) _____ and to

(**e**) _____ the same actions of the enemy army.

hypocrisy

VOCABULARY SKILLS 1 **Complete the table with the words in the box.**

~~with~~	of	at	for	lying	the truth
tax increases		~~murder~~		cheap labour	with

Verb	Preposition	Object
1 to charge s.o.	with	murder
2 to accuse s.o.		
3 to exploit a place		
4 to protest		
5 to present s.o.		

VOCABULARY SKILLS 2 **Use the verb, preposition, and noun combinations from Vocabulary skills 1 to complete the sentences. You may need to change some pronouns or verb forms.**

1 Everyone was shocked when the police arrested the old lady and _____.

2 Emma's face became red when her boss _____.

3 The textile company deny that they are _____ the region _____.

4 Many people surrounded the government building in order to _____.

5 Steve wouldn't listen to his friends' warning about his girlfriend, but when he saw her out with another guy, he was finally _____.

SPEAKING **Discuss the statements with a partner.**

1 We don't need gruesome photos of dead civilians in newspapers. Photos of people dying in war zones are simply voyeuristic. They don't make people feel more sympathetic, just curious.

2 Newspapers should not criticize the army of their own country. Soldiers have to go wherever they are sent by their country and do a good job. They need encouragement and praise, not criticism.

3 Most people don't really care about events in foreign countries. They feel so detached from these events that it is difficult to elicit their sympathy, particularly if they are inhabitants of wealthier countries.

Grammar	Look at the functions of *use/used to* below.
Use/Used to	**a** *The term 'blended family' can be used to replace 'Divorcees ...'*
	b *The use of euphemism is being exploited for far more sinister purposes.*
	c *We are now so used to double-speak that we are in danger of becoming truly desensitized.*
	d *I used to believe that war was about good versus evil.*

GRAMMAR 1 **Read the box above and answer the questions.**

  1 Which sentence shows *use* in the noun form?

  _____

  2 Which sentence has a passive form of *use*?

  _____

  3 Which sentence refers to a habit or situation in the past which is no longer true?

  _____

  4 Which sentence could be re-written with *familiar with*?

  _____

GRAMMAR 2 **Which sentences are correct? Re-write the incorrect sentences.**

  1 Learning a language well requires the use of a good dictionary.

  _____

  _____

  2 I regret that I never used to concentrating in my French classes.

  _____

  _____

  3 You'll have to get used to speak English all day if you work here.

  _____

  _____

  4 Euphemisms can be used in both formal and informal situations.

  _____

  _____

  5 When I studied in Australia, I couldn't get used the accent.

  _____

  _____

  6 I didn't used to like conversing in English, but it's got easier now.

  _____

  _____

Effective • *Skills*

INFERRING MEANING

You are going to read three interviews for an English language school magazine. Read the questions. Can you infer the meaning of the words in bold?

a Do you think culture has any **effect** on language?

b Which **aspect** of the English language is most challenging for you?

c How does learning English in an **Anglophone** country compare to learning English in your country?

d How important is the use of **gesture** as a means of supporting spoken communication?

e What would you say are the main differences in grammar between English and your **native** language?

f What do you do if an English speaker is talking too **rapidly**?

g Do you have any **tips** for learners of English from your country?

h What is your main **motivation** in learning English?

i Do people in your country think learning English is **worthwhile**?

j Can you tell me about a time when there was a **misunderstanding** between you and another English speaker?

SCANNING

Read the interviews quickly. Match the interviewer's questions above to each student's replies. (One question is not used.)

1 ___h___

2 _____

3 _____

4 _____

5 _____

6 _____

7 _____

8 _____

9 _____

Student *profile* page

This week we talk to Anastasia, Natalia, and Camilla to find out about their experiences of learning English.

Interviewer: How long have you been learning English?
Anastasia: Since I was five. My mother did an interpreting course at
5   university and she started teaching me English **from my young years**.

Interviewer: (1)_____?
Anastasia: Communication and reading. I love to read literature in the
author's own language. This has always **been very much fascinating**
for me. And, also communication because I want to talk to people and
10   it doesn't matter where I am there is always someone who can speak
English.

Interviewer: (2)_____?
Anastasia: Grammar! Yes, It really fascinates me, because you have so
many tenses and basically I have studied all of them but I can't always get
15   them right. And when I read the grammar or the vocabulary, I think 'yes I
know that', but when it **comes in terms of speaking** or writing I'm always
confused. Because I think 'Well maybe this will do' or 'I've read something
like this before' and sometimes I hit the bullseye and sometimes I can't
believe I could get it so wrong.
20

Interviewer: What do you think Russian students should know about
studying here?
Anastasia: Don't be afraid to talk. It doesn't matter if you make a mistake,
they'll explain. The **way to teach** is much more relaxed here.

Interviewer: (3)_____?
25   **Anastasia:** Nothing. I just need a few minutes to adjust and I'm usually OK.

> **Anastasia is organizing a meal at a
> Russian restaurant in Parnell this Saturday.
> If you want to go, put your name on the list
> in the Student Room.**

30

Interviewer: (4)_____?
Natalia: I think it's really different, because, like, I'm in a home-stay family
so I'm living with people from other countries. I'm living with a Swiss girl
and a Russian girl so it helps a lot because I have to speak English with
35   them and also, with the family I'm always speaking English, so it's really
challenging. In Brazil we speak Portuguese the whole time.

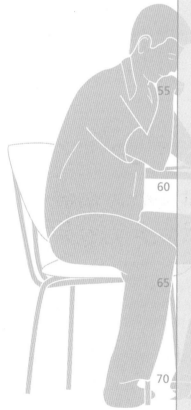

Interviewer: Do English and Portuguese have anything in common?
Natalia: Sometimes the words are pretty much the same. So visually you can **do the relation** between the English word and the Portuguese word. It doesn't always work though and sometimes you can get it wrong.

40

Interviewer: (5)_____?
Natalia: Oh, well I think they have to incorporate English into their lives as much as they can. Use songs, television, reading, anything. And try to go to an English-speaking country.

45

Interviewer: (6)_____?
Natalia: Definitely, I think that language is all the result of… Oh how can I say it? Language is a way of representing what a country… who the people are. That's the way I see it. I think they are totally connected. In Brazil, we… our sentences overlap, we often start talking before the other **people has finished**. And here I've noticed other people do that a tiny bit but nowhere near as much. So, sometimes conversations here seem to drag for me. I don't know.

50

> **Natalia has just finished the Teachers of English as a Second Language course. She's now going to take a well-deserved break in Fiji.**

55

Interviewer: Can you describe a typical English class in Sweden?
Camilla: The classes have about 20 students. All the four skills are important, and we do a lot of vocabulary and grammar. The teacher always stays in front of the class.

Interviewer: (7)_____?
Camilla: Absolutely. You know, you can speak English **in the whole world** and you can't speak Swedish. So for most of us it's vital.

60

Interviewer: (8)_____?
Camilla: Oh that's difficult. **It's a big difference.** But maybe one is, for example, the way we order our words in a sentence is quite different. In English, you can say 'I want to travel round the world' but we say 'round the world' first, and then 'I want to travel' after, so adverbs can go in different places.

65

Interviewer: (9)_____?
Camilla: Yes, one time **when I called to the hotel** to make a reservation, they didn't get what dates I wanted. When you speak face to face, it's easier. You can use gestures. But on the phone your pronunciation must be crystal clear.

70

> **Camilla is also hoping to improve her French while she's here. If you speak French and want to learn a little bit of Swedish, you can meet her in Room 5.**

**ERROR
CORRECTION**   The three students have a good level of English, but they made a few mistakes. Look again at the parts of the interviews in **bold**. Correct the mistakes using the following prompts.

For example:

from *when I was young.* _____

1   been very _____

2   it comes _____

3   teaching _____ more relaxed here

4   make the _____

5   people _____

6   speak English all _____

7   There are _____

8   one time when I _____ to make a reservation

DISCUSSION   Interview a partner with some of the questions from Inferring meaning on page 12.

WRITING   Write a reply to an email from an English-speaking friend who is trying to learn your language before coming to work in your country. First read part of the email.

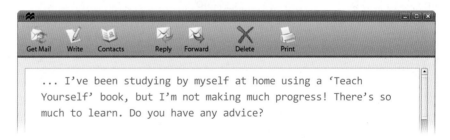

- Describe your experience of being a language learner.
- Suggest other ways that your friend could learn your language.
- Say what areas of your language your friend should focus on.

2 • Local culture

PRE-READING 1 You are going to read a text about the experiences of four travellers. Use your dictionary to find the meaning of these words and write in the definitions and translations. All the words appear in the text.

Word/Phrase	Definition	Translation
1 liberal (*adj*)	_____	_____
2 vast (*adj*)	_____	_____
3 to bear a relation to	_____	_____
4 to dress down	_____	_____
5 to depict	_____	_____
6 to co-exist	_____	_____
7 courteous (*adj*)	_____	_____

PRE-READING 2 Which cultural features do you think the travellers mention for each of the following countries? Choose two features from the box for each country.

liberal attitude to behaviour   different nationalities co-existing spoken language bears no relation to written   dressing down tiles depicting scenes from history   vast plates of meat similar apartment buildings   courteous waiters

1 Portugal   2 the United States   3 Brazil   4 England

Read the text and review your answers.

Travellers' tales

The Internet may make it easier to chat to our global neighbours, but the world still holds surprises for travellers. In this month's edition of Working Overseas, *we speak to four people about their experiences in a foreign country.*

A Jeff Stevens

Originally from a small farming town in the midwest of the United States, Jeff surfed the net to find his first teaching job. He was lucky almost straight away, finding a full-time job in Lisbon, the capital of Portugal, but he took a while to get used to the language. 'I'd tried to study Portuguese before I arrived and I was doing pretty well, but when I got to Lisbon I found that the sounds bore no relation to the words on the page. After a month or two, I really **got into it** and stopped feeling like a complete alien. By the time I left, I could communicate well enough to get by.' Coming from a relatively new country, Jeff was impressed by the importance the Portuguese place on their past. 'In the old parts of the city, the houses are covered with beautifully illustrated tiles depicting famous scenes from past centuries. The locals are very proud of them and lots of my students would take me on walking tours to show me their favourites. I can't see many Americans spending time showing visitors around their cities, at least, not for free.'

B Jane Hilton

Taking a break from her job in Australia, Jane packed her bags for the United States, initially for a holiday. She started off in California where she found it was 'a lot less liberal than I'd expected'. She explains, 'I was on the beach and took off my top. A lifeguard immediately came zooming along on a scooter and told me it was a $90 instant fine. Anyway, he **let me off** because I was a foreigner,' she laughs. And what other cultural differences did Jane **come up against**? 'When I was trying to get waitressing work, I didn't have a car and was quite intimidated at the thought of driving on the freeway – it's too fast and they drive on the other side of the road!' So she looked around for a bus, but found there weren't any. 'Apparently, a petrochemical company had bought the whole transport system and then **phased it out**. In the end, I walked long distances, which was another strange thing to do, and got **told off** again – this time by a cop for loitering, when in actual fact I was just standing there.' And how did Jane get on at work? 'American waiters and waitresses are very courteous, so I was probably more abrupt and straightforward and a bit of a novelty, and I got good tips. It was interesting because people I'd barely laid eyes on were prepared to tell me the most amazingly private things – about their

divorces and breast augmentations, for example. Australians would
find that really weird! Despite my problems, though, I had a great
45   time in the States. The American 'can-do' attitude is very infectious
and the people ooze positivity.'

C Martin McMorrow

Despite his London roots, Martin found himself quite disoriented in
the even bigger city of São Paulo, Brazil. 'There are so many similar
50   apartment buildings, you don't get a sense of where you are,' he
says, 'and it's very difficult to find the bus stops because most of
them are just small, green, wooden poles with nothing written on
them. For a long time, the routes were a complete mystery!' Martin
still managed to find his way to the local *churrascaria* restaurant
55   where the waiters come round with vast plates of meat. 'You have
this little disc on your table. If you turn up the green side, they come
and serve you. When you're full, you turn it over to red and it
means, stop, I'm about to explode!' Martin also quickly adapted to
the Brazilian habit of **heading for** the beach every weekend.
60   However, there was one aspect of beach culture that he found rather
unusual. 'People will try to sell you anything, like normal
umbrellas – which is the last thing you'd want at the beach – or
clothes or electrical goods, and you don't even have your wallet, so it
seems a bit optimistic! But a really nice thing was the coconut
65   milk – they chop off the top and give you a straw!'

D Guiliana Silveira

Guiliana went to England to take a two-week course for foreign
teachers of English, but ended up staying for ten years. 'I fell in love
with London and decided to stay there!' she explains. 'I remember
70   the first time I went to Camden Town, I was just in awe of all the
different looks. You can dress down, be eccentric, be a punk, and no
one bats an eyelid.' Another aspect of London life that Guiliana
found different was its multi-cultural population. 'I've never seen so
many different nationalities, and from places I'd never heard of!
75   People seemed to co-exist really well then, whereas now I feel that
people are a bit more suspicious of each other. That's a pity.' Guiliana
was also astounded by the number of charity shops in the high
streets. 'It's not very common at all in Brazil to buy used stuff. You
donate it to schools and they take it to the poor. For me, that was
80   quite unique to London.'

COMPREHENSION 1 **Read the text and answer the questions.**

Which traveller ...

1 was impressed with the way people were indifferent to each other's appearance?

2 likes the nation's attitude towards its history?

3 explains a custom associated with a type of service?

4 was reluctant to travel in the way other people did?

5 took some time to be able to understand what people were saying?

6 compares two approaches to the recycling of second-hand goods?

7 was surprised at the way strangers confided personal information?

8 expresses surprise at the kind of goods sold at the beach?

9 mentions a change they observed in the attitude to people from other countries?

10 appreciates the decorations on the buildings?

11 gives reasons for getting lost in the city he or she went to?

12 unknowingly behaved in a way that was prohibited?

COMPREHENSION 2 **Answer the questions.**

1 In line 9, which phrase means *to become familiar with*?

2 In line 14, what is the best translation for *to get by*?

    a To communicate in very basic language.

    b To be able to understand enough to live fairly easily.

    c To speak and understand very well.

3 In lines 14-15, what is meant by *a relatively new country*?

    A country which ...

    a has long-established traditions and culture.

    b has a genuine love for the royal family.

    c has quite a short history.

4 In lines 19-20, which phrase means *I am unable to imagine*?

5 In line 28, what is the meaning o-f *let me off*?

    The police officer ...

    a didn't punish me.

    b didn't let me leave.

    c didn't like me because I was a foreigner.

6 In line 37, the function of *in actual fact* is to show ...

    a the order of events.

    b the reality.

    c the specific place.

7 In line 41, what is meant by *people I'd barely laid eyes on?*

    a People I didn't really trust.

    b Customers I'd seen a few times before.

    c People I'd only just met.

8 What does Jane Hilton suggest about Americans in her final comment?

    a There is a high rate of infectious disease in the United States, but people are happy.

    b People have a very positive outlook to life and show it in their attitude.

    c She enjoyed herself because of her positive outlook, despite the problems she encountered.

9 In line 48, what does the word *roots* mean?

    a destinations   **b** origins   **c** residences

10 In lines 63-64, what is meant by *it seems a bit optimistic*?

    a There is a good chance of finding whatever you want to buy.

    b The sellers are charging an unreasonable amount for the goods.

    c It is unlikely that anyone could sell these types of goods.

11 In line 70, what is the best replacement for *in awe of*?
I thought the looks were ...

    a confusing.   **b** amusing.   **c** amazing.

12 In lines 71-72, what is meant by *no one bats an eyelid*?
No one ...

    a copies you.   **b** is shocked.   **c** ignores you.

VOCABULARY SKILLS 1

Find the phrasal verbs in bold in the text. Match them to the following definitions (1–6).

1 To give someone little or no punishment for something they did wrong

2 To go in a particular direction

3 To start enjoying something or become enthusiastic about it

4 To gradually stop doing something

5 To face or deal with something difficult or unpleasant

6 To criticize someone angrily for doing something wrong

To start enjoying something or become enthusiastic about it.

VOCABULARY SKILLS 2   **Complete the sentences with the correct form of the phrasal verbs from Vocabulary skills 1.**

1   The last time I saw Eric he was _____ the bus stop.

2   My mother used to _____ me _____ for hitting my sister.

3   The government is _____ free travel for the elderly.

4   When I lived in Germany, I really _____ opera!

5   Our team _____ some tough competition next month.

6   Most first-time young offenders are _____ with a warning.

Grammar

Although/Despite/ However

Although I've travelled by plane many times, I still hate flying!
Although connects two clauses and requires a comma after the clause.

Despite traveling by plane many times, I still hate flying.
Despite connects two clauses and requires a comma after the clause. It is followed by a noun, an -*ing* form, or *the fact that* + subject, verb, object.

I've travelled by plane many times, **however**, I still hate flying.
I've travelled by plane many times. **However**, I still hate flying.
However connects two clauses or two sentences and requires a comma after it.

GRAMMAR   **Choose the correct words to complete the sentences.**

1   Jeff enjoyed his time in Portugal, *although / despite* he had some problems with the language.

2   *Despite the fact that / However,* he is American himself, Jeff is slightly critical of Americans.

3   Jane committed an offence in San Francisco. *However / Although*, she was let off because she was a foreigner.

4   Jane committed an offence in San Francisco. She was, *however / although*, let off because she was a foreigner.

5   Martin quickly adapted to the Brazilian habit of heading for the beach every weekend. *Although / Despite this*, there was one aspect of beach culture he found rather unusual.

6   *Although / Despite* Martin quickly adapted to the Brazilian habit of heading for the beach every weekend, there was one aspect of beach culture he found rather unusual.

7   *Despite / However* coming from London, Martin found himself quite disorientated in São Paulo.

8   Martin found himself quite disorientated in São Paulo *although / however* he came from London.

SPEAKING   **You want to tell a foreign visitor about your country. What would you say about:**

- transport   • eating out   • behaviour in public   • tipping
- festivals   • well-known figures that many people admire

Effective • *Skills*

ACTIVATING
KNOWLEDGE **What do you know about fair trade and free trade, and the effect they have on culture? Complete the sentences with fair trade or free trade.**

1 Consumers buy _____ products for ethical reasons.

2 _____ products often have misleading pictures on the packaging.

3 Coffee was the first commodity to be sold under the _____ system.

4 Under the _____ system, buyers have to pay producers more than the market price.

5 _____ enables small-scale farmers to stay in business.

6 _____ can create bad working conditions for employees.

7 Consumers pay more for _____ products than _____ products.

8 _____ helps indigenous people remain in a community.

**INFERRING
MEANING** **Find the words in bold in the text. Read the surrounding sentence(s) and then match the words to the following definitions.**

1 A symbol that represents an organization or company, used for example in its advertisements or on its products

2 The act of not buying or using something as a protest

3 A way of tricking or confusing someone in order to make them do what you want

4 An amount of money paid in addition to the usual amount

5 People who have lived in a place for a long time before other people arrived

6 Something that can be bought and sold

When you buy your coffee, what brand do you automatically reach for? Are you motivated by your taste buds, the weekly budget, or a commercial with deeply-satisfied espresso drinkers? In fact, according to recent customer feedback at Citymarket stores, it's definitely a question of promotion. Now, however, there is a fourth motive: the ethical choice. Many brands of coffee now come packaged in jars or packets illustrated with the joyful faces of Latin American labourers or African farmers. This is a deliberate marketing **ploy** to mislead you into thinking your purchase is contributing in some way to their economic well-being, when in fact, you are just adding to the profits of a multinational corporation. It is this kind of hypocrisy that the Fairtrade Labelling Organizations International (FLO) is attempting to expose.

The Fairtrade group was established in 1997 with a view to ensuring, as the name suggests, a fair deal for producers in developing countries. Coffee was the first **commodity** to be sold under the Fairtrade label, and the range has now extended to cocoa, chocolate, honey, rice, and wine. If a company wants to use the Fairtrade label for one of its products, it must agree to pay producers above the market price, and to also pay a small **premium**. This money allows small-scale farmers and co-operatives to stay in business when transnational companies are selling at lower prices. Sales reached $2 billion last year – a drop in the ocean compared to the revenue that free-trade products bring in – but an increase in sales nonetheless, and a clear indication that consumers are becoming increasingly aware of the conditions under which the items in their trolley are produced. Paying a little extra for a jar of coffee or a bar of chocolate will not really dent the wallets of shoppers in industrialized countries, but it makes a huge difference to those in the country of origin.

Many corporations are beginning to see that demonstrating a sense of social responsibility is good for business, and they know that consumer awareness can affect their profit margins. This is why British retailer Marks & Spencer has begun to sell Fairtrade clothes from India, why Ben and Jerry's ice cream

30 | now comes in Fairtrade Vanilla, and why Nestlé has launched Nestlé Nescafé Partners Blend, clearly marked with the Fairtrade **logo**.

Nevertheless, the reality for many workers in developing countries is still sweatshop conditions and little hope of escaping the cycle of poverty. This is the dark side of free trade that orthodox economists are willing to ignore.
35 | Companies know they can greatly increase their profits by setting up factories in developing countries. They can lower production costs by avoiding the minimum wage, health and safety practices, working hours and employees' rights. It is often only through the efforts of human rights organizations that these conditions are exposed. Both Gap and Nike were threatened with a
40 | consumer **boycott** for this very reason.

Trade Aid is another company that seeks to promote local sustainability for **indigenous** people and a sense of pride in their cultural traditions. From Trade Aid shops you can buy masks, jewellery, wooden and stone carvings, hand-woven textiles, and other handicrafts; all crafted by artisans in exactly the same
45 | way that their ancestors did. Like Fairtrade products, these goods are not inexpensive, but that's the point: you know the producers have not been exploited. For rural communities in countries such as Peru, Bolivia, Kenya, Ethiopia, and South Africa, to name but a few, the money from this industry allows families to stay together. The alternative is for members to migrate in
50 | search of domestic or seasonal work, causing community disintegration.

Little by little, Fairtrade is rewriting the rules of business to ensure that everyone can profit from worldwide trade.

SCANNING **Read the text as quickly as possible and review your answers to Activating knowledge on page 22.**

ANALYZING MEANING **Decide if the information about the text is True (T), False (F), or Not Given (NG). Write T, F, or NG.**

1 Consumers at Citymarket stores choose coffee according to cost. ☐

2 Coffee does not always come from the country you think it does. ☐

3 When Fairtrade was first set up, its producers had to make some changes to their methods of production. ☐

4 In the previous year, sales of Fairtrade products went up. ☐

5 Marks & Spencer's profits have increased as a result of selling Fairtrade clothes. ☐

6 Companies choose developing countries that have no laws regarding the conditions and pay of workers. ☐

7 Trade Aid producers are using new techniques to produce crafts. ☐

8 Some people have returned to their community in order to work for Trade Aid. ☐

VOCABULARY EXTENSION

Find a word, phrase, or expression in the text that matches the definitions.

1 The satisfactory state that someone or something should be in (involving such things as happiness, money, health, safety). (lines 5-11) _____

2 To deliberately make something known publicly because you believe it to be wrong or illegal. (lines 5-11) _____

3 The intention of doing something in the future. (lines 12-15) _____

4 A very small amount that will not have much effect. (lines 17-23) _____

5 A factory where people work very hard in bad conditions and earn very little money. (lines 32-34) _____

6 The condition of being completely destroyed by breaking something into lots of very small pieces. (lines 49-52) _____

DISCUSSION

Discuss the questions with a partner.

Fairtrade products are mainly bought by the 25-40 age group.

1 Why do you think other age groups are not so interested in these products?

2 What do you think Fairtrade should do to widen its appeal?

3 In which ways could Fairtrade be used in your country?

WRITING

Write an email to the dean of your college or university.

• You would like Fairtrade products to be available at your college or university.

• Explain what Fairtrade does.

• Suggest what kind of products students would be interested in.

• Say how or where the products could be sold.

EXERCISE 1

EXERCISE 1

Read the text.

Is language unique to humans?

According to Dr Sue Savage-Rumbaugh at Georgia State University, humans are not the only species capable of language. She carried out an extensive training and testing programme with a bonobo chimpanzee called Kanzi, who, by the age of six, had mastered a vocabulary of 200 words along with a series of meaningful gestures. (Since chimpanzees, like all primates, lack vocal chords, Kanzi was taught to use a keyboard and press symbols as a means of communicating.) The testing also involved commands being given by hidden speakers, so the research team could affirm that Kanzi was not just responding to contextual cues. It was reported that Kanzi responded accurately to 74 per cent of the complex questions that were put to him.

However, there are many who are far from convinced by this research. Among them is linguist Noam Chomsky who believes that only humans possess the innate cognitive ability to both comprehend and produce language. He compares human children with apes: the former learn to speak rapidly and can produce original sentences, but the primates find even the learning of a few words extremely challenging. Furthermore, Chomsky states that the ability to use individual symbols does not equate to the ability to recognize syntax. Cognitive scientist Steven Pinker is also sceptical and believes that Kanzi has merely learnt to behave in a way that will earn him a reward. In another experiment with a chimp called Washoe, his trainers were convinced he was capable of using American Sign Language. But Pinker points to the fact that a deaf researcher who studied Washoe reported that the chimp was not using sign language, but actually his own set of gestures.

EXERCISE 2

Complete the sentences with words from the text. Write no more than two words for each answer.

1 Dr Savage-Rumbaugh claimed Kanzi used _____, as well as vocabulary, to communicate.

2 Kanzi was given a keyboard to communicate with as chimpanzees do not possess _____.

3 _____ were used to make sure Kanzi could understand language without the support of visual information.

4 According to Noam Chomsky, primates cannot understand and use language as they do not have naturally occurring _____.

5 Chomsky believes that the use of _____ is not evidence of understanding how language works.

6 Steven Pinker uses the observations of a _____ to discredit the idea of a chimp using sign language.

EXERCISE 1

Read the text.

Social customs

How many people, whether on business abroad or merely touring, have unknowingly insulted their clients, hosts, local shopkeepers, or a complete stranger on the bus? A quick read of our guide below will help you to conform to social norms and make a positive impression.

First, behaving in the same way that you would at home can land you in fairly serious trouble. In England, it is standard practice to take wine to a dinner party, but the same does not apply in France. To do so would suggest your host is unable to choose or afford a good bottle. If you are doing business in Turkey, be careful who you speak to first. Age is seen as evidence of wisdom and therefore you should start with the oldest person in the room. Some Turkish people also consider it disrespectful for young people to cross their legs in front of older people, something most westerners wouldn't even think about.

In some countries, your body language may be unwittingly offensive. Do not pat girls or boys on the head in Thailand as this is considered the most sacred part of the body, and make sure the soles of your feet are not on display in Arab countries. It is important to bow lower than your seniors or elders in Japan, and elderly members of Maori tribes in New Zealand would find your bottom resting on a table or desk to be extremely disrespectful.

As for everyday behaviour on the street, if you have a cold, turn away from others and use your tissues discreetly in Germany. Never step over a coin or a note in Thailand. These bear the image of the king and are therefore deserving of respect.

When you are indoors, don't light up in Canada without first asking permission, and in Arab countries, it would be unthinkable to walk into a house with footwear on.

EXERCISE 2

Answer the questions as quickly as possible.

In which country/countries should you ...

1 hide the bottom of your feet?

2 ask if it is OK to smoke inside?

3 avoid walking over money?

4 avoid sitting on tables?

5 avoid touching someone's head?

6 speak to the oldest person first in a business meeting?

7 avoid taking wine to dinner parties?

8 avoid crossing your legs in front of older people?

9 remove your shoes before entering a house?

10 blow your nose privately?

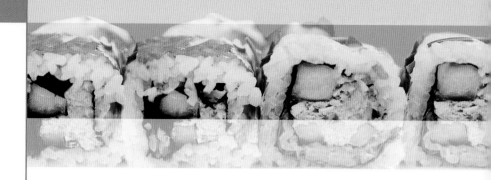

3 • Food

PRE-READING 1 **You are going to read about food from different countries. Choose the correct meaning for the following words. The words are in bold in the text.**

1 *an acquired taste*

   a food or drink that takes a long time to prepare

   b something that you do not like at first, but gradually start to enjoy

   c a dish that is healthy, but doesn't taste very pleasant

2 *to preserve something*

   a to improve the taste of food

   b to keep food fresh for a long time

   c to put something in a place unknown to others

3 *open-minded (adj)*

   a very imaginative

   b able to control your thoughts

   c willing to accept new ideas

4 *to ban something*

   a to say officially that people must not do, sell, or use something

   b to form an agreement between two groups

   c to provide information and advice on a subject

PRE-READING 2 **Read the descriptions quickly. Match the following countries (1–6) to a paragraph (A–F).**

1 Russia = _____

2 New Zealand = _____

3 Japan = _____

4 the United States = _____

5 Nicaragua = _____

6 Italy = _____

International travellers shouldn't miss ...

A The Hot Dog Eating Contest (in _____)
This contest takes place every year. This summer, 20 contestants are taking part. The winner will be the person who eats the most hot dogs and buns in 12 minutes. It may surprise you that being overweight is a drawback. It is far more important to have 'an elastic stomach', so the competitors train by drinking lots of water in a very short time to make their stomachs stretch. Sometimes, they quickly dip the buns in water to make them easier to swallow. Although most competitors are local US citizens, Japanese Takeru 'Tsunami' Kobayashi currently holds the world record: he ate 53 ½ hot dogs on 4 July, 2004! There is no cash prize for this contest: the winner receives a mustard-yellow belt and a year's supply of hot dogs.

B Ricci di Mare (from _____)
Don't worry! No one will actually expect you to eat the spines of the 'Ricci di Mare'. What people love most about these spiky sea urchins is the 'roe' that is inside. It has a strong salty flavour and some may find it **an acquired taste**. All around the coast of this country, famous for its delicious food and wine, you will find these prickly sea creatures. You can eat it with spaghetti in a lemon sauce or even buy it **preserved** in jars from delicatessens. However, the locals think it's best to simply collect it from the rock pools at low tide and eat it right on the beach.

C The Wildfoods Festival (in _____)
The festival takes place in the old mining town of Hokitika on the west coast of the South Island. This year, the organizers are preparing for more than 23,000 curious visitors from all over the world, a 10 per cent increase in attendance over last year's crowd. Each year, the chefs invent more and more exotic dishes, and you may need to have a strong stomach and be **open-minded** to try them. This year they are offering new dishes such as insect eggs, scorpions, and venison tongue. Last year's favourites are still available: kangaroo and emu steaks fresh from neighbouring Australia, and of course, earthworms and snails. It's a country full of sheep, but don't expect to eat any of them here!

D A very big beer can (in _____)
When was the last time you drank beer that came out of a petrol tanker at the side of the road? Well, in the land of the Tsars, you can. Kvass is a weak beer made from fermented rye bread, and, yes, it is sold by the glass and only from big yellow tankers in towns and

40 cities all over the country, although the best is said to come from Zvenigorod. It's not expensive and locals insist that it is the best thing in the world on a hot summer's day and will even protect you from infectious diseases.

E The blow fish (from _____)

45 This is usually a very expensive fish and a special dish. A chef needs special training and skill to prepare the dish properly since there are parts of the fish that are very poisonous and can kill a customer almost immediately. To make it even more difficult, the location of the poisonous parts varies among different types of blow fish. There 50 is no medicine or cure for blow fish poisoning. In fact, it is the only food the emperor is not allowed to eat. People who love blow fish say the most poisonous ones are also the most delicious! Nowadays, blow fish is becoming a more popular dish, so you can even buy prepared blow fish in supermarkets and on websites.

F Iguana stew (from _____)

55 Because the iguana is a rare species, the government now completely **bans** people from hunting them from 1 December to 31 March. After that, it isn't difficult to find iguana stew in the market, especially at Easter, when it is a traditional dish. People eat 60 iguanas for several reasons. During Lent, many Catholics abstain from eating meat. Iguanas are nutritious and people also believe they have medicinal powers. If you look in a 65 cooking pot, you can see pieces of iguana (perhaps a whole head, feet and claws, bits of body, the tail, and some skin) as well as 70 vegetables or rice. Unfortunately for the iguana, the legal ban does not extend across other Central or Latin American 75 countries.

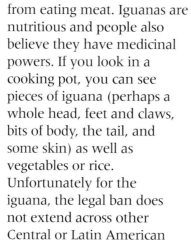

COMPREHENSION 1   **Decide if the information about the text is True (T), False (F), or Not Given (NG). Write T, F, or NG.**

1   Fatter people are more likely to win the hot dog contest. ☐

2   Contestants drink a lot of water during the contest. ☐

3   Most tourists like Ricci di Mare with pasta. ☐

4   More people are expected to attend this year's Wildfoods Festival. ☐

5   This year's Wildfoods Festival dishes are replacing the favourite dishes from last year. ☐

6   People do not buy Kvass in cans. ☐

7   Drinkers of Kvass claim it is good for your health. ☐

8   Different kinds of blow fish have different poisonous parts. ☐

9   Hunters in this country still catch iguanas illegally. ☐

10   Some people believe iguana meat can help them recover from illness. ☐

COMPREHENSION 2   **Answer the questions.**

1   What is the closest synonym for *drawback* (line 5)?

   a   technique

   b   attraction

   c   disadvantage

2   What is the best definition for *spines* in line 14?

   a   sharp points

   b   hard skin

   c   shells

3   In line 16, what does *it* refer to?

4   In line 38, the word *yes* suggests that ...

   a   you can't buy beer in the countryside.

   b   Kvass is a weak beer.

   c   buying beer from tankers is unusual.

5   In line 43, the word *infectious* means ...

   a   very painful and possibly fatal.

   b   easy to spread from one person to another.

   c   familiar to doctors in poor countries.

6   In line 46, what can you replace *since* with?

   a   from   b   because   c   after

7 In line 48, what does *it* refer to?

   a the training the chef requires

   b the treatment for poison

   c the preparation of the fish

8 In line 69, what is the function of *as well as*?

   a It shows addition.

   b It is followed by an example.

   c It shows another possibility.

VOCABULARY SKILLS 1

Complete the sentences with the words in the box.

since	in order to	in fact	as well as

1 Eating fast food once in a while isn't, _____ , so bad for your health.

2 You need to go on a strict diet _____ lose weight.

3 If you want to lose weight you need to eat less _____ exercise more.

4 My room-mate does most of the cooking for us _____ I can't cook.

VOCABULARY SKILLS 2

Make collocations with the words in bold and the options below.

1 (from A) **overweight**

   child   traffic   baggage   animal

2 (from C) **exotic**

   location   CD   costume   software program

3 (from C) **-minded**

   narrow   closed   broad   wide

4 (from F) **rare**

   time   book   plant   -looking person

exotic

overweight

rare

Grammar	Look at the reasons we use the present simple.
Present simple	**a** to describe permanent situations
	b to explain routines/habits/regular events
	c with stative verbs
	d to express facts
	e for timetables

GRAMMAR 1 Write a reason from the box above (a–e) next to a suitable example below.

Reason	Example
1	The sea urchin's roe has a strong salty flavour.
2	The festival starts at 9am and finishes at 7pm.
3	The Hot Dog Eating Contest takes place every year.
4	Catholics abstain from eating meat during Lent.
5	Kvass is a weak beer.

Grammar	Look at the reasons we use the present progressive.
Present progressive	**a** to describe what's happening at the time we're speaking
	b to describe temporary situations
	c to show a development or trend
	d to talk about arrangements or decisions (made in the past for the future)

GRAMMAR 2 Write a reason from the box above (a–d) next to a suitable example below.

Reason	Example
1	I'm working as a waitress while I look for a better job.
2	Sorry, can you phone me again later? I'm cooking dinner now.
3	20 contestants are taking part this year.
4	Around the world, governments are becoming more concerned about endangered species.

Effective • *Skills*

Answer the questions.

1 You visit the home of an English-speaking friend. On the kitchen table is a pot of coffee. Your friend says, 'Help yourself.'

Is your friend ...

a feeling tired?

b expecting you to say no?

c being friendly?

2 It's your birthday and you take some cakes to work to share. Your colleague Stephanie says to you, 'Don't offer them to Nicole first! She's so greedy!'

What does Stephanie mean?

a Nicole eats more than she needs.

b Nicole is overweight.

c Nicole would disapprove of eating during work time.

3 Your room-mate comes back from the supermarket and starts to complain, 'I hate buying food that has so much packaging!' What is your room-mate unhappy about?

a the flavours that are added to food

b the plastic, boxes, etc. round the food

c the chemicals that make the food last longer

4 You're staying with some American friends. It's nearly dinner time, but everyone is too tired to do the cooking. Brad says, 'What about those pizzas? Were there any leftovers?' What is Brad suggesting?

a Maybe we could finish the pizzas that we started eating yesterday.

b Perhaps we have enough money to get a pizza delivered to our house.

c We could eat the pizzas if everyone likes all the ingredients.

SCANNING   **Quickly read A–D on page 35 and answer the questions.**

Which of the sections (A–D) ...

1 describes a national custom? _____

2 is spoken by a student/students? _____

3 explains a new trend? _____

4 gives advice? _____ and _____

5 describes behaviour between good friends? _____

Bad habits?

A

'When my friends and I go out to eat, we often take food from each other's plates. It's a good way of seeing what different food tastes like. We just use our own fork and take a little bit – maybe some pasta or cake. Of course, the friend has to say, 'This is really good! You should have some,' first. You can't just go
5 ahead and help yourself. And don't be greedy! Oh, and these are friends that you've known for ages. It can't just be a work colleague.'

B

'If you go somewhere to eat with your boyfriend or girlfriend, people from my country think it's romantic to feed each other. Maybe people of my grandparents' generation will frown at you, but I think it was just the same in
10 their day. So, I mean, if you're eating ice cream or something like that, you can use your own spoon to feed him or her a little bit. And just do it once or twice … not the whole meal!'

C

'What we usually do for lunch is go to a café where they serve lots of little dishes and everyone helps himself or herself. There's really loads of food and we never
15 finish everything. The service is fast, too. There is one thing, though. I'm pretty sure they use the leftovers to serve to the next group of customers. I don't mind too much. It's cheap and I don't have a lot of money at the moment, and it's quick, which is good because we have to hurry back for the afternoon lecture.'

D

Jenny: What are you reading about?
20 **Martin:**   Oh, it's an article on freeganism.
Jenny: What's that? I've never heard of it.
Martin: Well, some people believe that our society wastes too much stuff.
               They think we should eat food that supermarkets throw away.
Jenny: You mean they get it out of dustbins? That sounds disgusting!
25 **Martin:**   Yes, but the food's still in its packaging and there's nothing wrong
               with it. They just throw it away on the day of the sell-by date. The
               writer says he gets some good meals that way.
Jenny: Maybe, but those cans are really dirty. I'm sure freegans must get
               food poisoning a lot.
30 **Martin:**   Maybe. He doesn't say he's been ill, though.
Jenny: Well, I can't imagine this idea is going to become very popular.
Martin: I don't know, but I admire people for having strong beliefs.
Jenny: Are you planning to become a freegan?
Martin: Er, maybe not!

UNDERSTANDING
ATTITUDE AND
OPINION

Read A–D on page 35 more carefully and answer the questions below.

A

1 Why does the speaker take food from his/her friends' plates?

   a It's a way of saving money.

   b It's a way of trying new dishes.

B

2 What does the speaker mean by *I think it was just the same in their day*?

   a You can see people behaving like this many times during the day.

   b Older people behaved like this when they were young.

C

3 What does the speaker think the café does with leftover food?

   a Sells it more cheaply to students.

   b Gives it to other customers.

4 How does the speaker feel about this?

   a unconcerned

   b disgusted

D

5 What do freegans believe?

   a Supermarkets should not put good food in dustbins.

   b The products in supermarkets are overpriced.

6 Does Martin persuade Jenny that freeganism is a good way of living? Underline the parts of the text that help you decide.

7 When Martin says, 'Er, maybe not!' Do you think he is …

   a angry with Jenny?

   b quite embarrassed?

   c telling a lie?

DISCUSSION 1 **What do you think about the behaviour the speakers describe in A–D? Tick (✔) the statements that you agree with.**

☐ It's OK to take food from your friends' plates.

☐ It's OK to feed your boyfriend or girlfriend in a restaurant.

☐ It's OK for restaurants to serve leftovers to other customers.

☐ Freegans have a good way of finding their food.

Now discuss your opinions with a partner.

DISCUSSION 2   **Use the words in the box to complete the dialogues. Two words are not used. Practise the dialogues with a partner.**

stuff	leftovers	sell-by date	help
disgusting	loads	greedy	

1   A: Could I try a little bit of that cheesecake, please?

   B: Yes. _____ yourself.

2   A: I've just invented a new drink made of Coke and yoghurt!

   B: Sounds _____!

3   A: We've run out of cat food.

   B: Well, use the _____ from last night's dinner then.

4   A: Do you want any more to eat?

   B: No, thanks. I've eaten _____ already. I'm full.

5   A: Is this milk OK to drink? It smells a bit funny.

   B: I don't know. Check the _____.

PRONUNCIATION   **Mark the words in the sentences that have the most stress. Remember to put the stress over the correct syllable, too.**

1   Oh, it's an article on freeganism.

2   Well, some people believe that our society wastes too much stuff.

3   You mean they get it out of dustbins? That sounds disgusting!

4   Maybe, but those bins are really dirty.

5   I'm sure freegans must get food poisoning a lot.

6   Well, I can't imagine this idea is going to become very popular.

4 • Film

PRE-READING **Match the words in bold in sentences 1–8 to the correct definitions (a–h).**

1 Julia Roberts is a very experienced actress. She has at least 45 films and TV shows in her **filmography**.   _f_

2 That film was so **predictable**. We knew how it would end after the first five minutes.   ____

3 The **reviewers** were very critical of his latest film but the audiences loved it.   ____

4 You would have to be a total **psychopath** to be so cruel and so violent.   ____

5 When he was younger, George Clooney was always **typecast** as the romantic Interest, but now he plays lots of different roles.   ____

6 When Leonardo DiCaprio and Kate Winslet acted together in *Titanic*, there was real **chemistry** between them.   ____

7 Science fiction isn't a **genre** I'm interested in. I prefer horror!   ____

8 Some actors have very good **diction** but others just mumble and it's really hard to understand them.   ____

a a particular style used in film, writing or art

b an adjective that means you know in advance what will happen

c a person suffering from a serious mental illness that causes them to behave in a violent way towards other people

d always being given the same kind of character to play in film or theatre

e the way that someone pronounces words

f a list of the films or TV programmes that an actor has appeared in

g people who give their opinion of films, books, restaurants etc. in newspapers, magazines or on the Internet

h the relationship between two people, which often includes a strong sexual attraction

Foreign stars hit and miss in Hollywood

There aren't many actors round the world who have enough self-confidence to turn down an offer from Steven Spielberg. Maybe that was why Juliette Binoche gave him a choice. She said she'd be happy to be in *Jurassic Park* as long as she could play a dinosaur. Of
5   course he turned her down and it was probably a good thing. It's difficult to imagine Juliette ripping people apart with her teeth. However, her decision doesn't seem to have done her career any harm. She has gone on to make a string of hits, including *The Unbearable Lightness of Being*, *The English Patient* (for which she won
10   an Oscar), and *Chocolat*.

Success in the United States has not been so easy for other foreign stars. Gérard Depardieu is a good example. Since his first film in 1967, his filmography lists 172 acting credits. But he has struggled on the other side of the pond. While some of his films have been
15   popular in the US, they have usually been French films that travelled. One possible exception was *Green Card*, directed by Peter Weir, where he plays a French immigrant who goes through a fake wedding in order to stay and work in the United States. This is a predictable but sweet romantic comedy which typecasts its lead
20   actors in terms of national stereotypes. While some reviewers were kind, others shredded both the film and Depardieu's performance.

While Monsieur Depardieu hasn't received the recognition he would have liked in the United States, one Mexican actor has achieved almost instant success. Gael García Bernal first gained recognition in
25   *Amores Perros* in 2000 and a year later in *Y tu mamá también*. Since then he has appeared with hometown hero, Brad Pitt in *Babel* and, under the direction of top producer and director, Jim Jarmusch, he starred in *Limits of Control*. He hasn't picked up an Oscar yet,
30   but he was nominated for a BAFTA in 2005 for his performance as the South American hero revolutionary, Che Guevara, in *Motorcycle Diaries*. In the same year he
35   played American music icon Elvis Presley in *The King*.

40 Of course every now and again a foreign actor will capture the imagination of both the audience and the critics. Anyone who has seen *No Country for Old Men* will find it difficult to forget Javier Bardem's monosyllabic psychopath with bad hair. Bardem has got off to a great start, but he didn't have to say much in this film. So the big question is whether he'll get the lead in a major Hollywood production. There is certainly chemistry between him and Penelope Cruz in *Vicky Cristina Barcelona*, which has led to much speculation in the gossip columns as to whether they are an item or not. The problem for Bardem is that he now needs a really big hit to consolidate his success so far.

45

50 Maybe the one genre where foreign actors have an edge is in action films. For Jean-Claude Van Damme (the Muscles from Brussels), a solid grounding in kick boxing was much more useful than good diction. US audiences were fascinated by his trademark 360 degree kick to his opponent's head in *Bloodsport* in 1988 and it has kept him employed ever since. Even if your action hero does have to speak, a foreign accent is usually seen as an asset. Just think of Arnie Schwarzenegger, governor of California. American voters have promoted him from action hero to leader of the largest economy in the United States. But a whole generation of people will remember him primarily as The Terminator. Perhaps the next wave of foreign actors heading for Hollywood will break the cycle and be treated on their acting merits. If not, maybe more will go into politics.

55

60

COMPREHENSION 1 **Answer the questions.**

1 Does the writer infer that Juliette Binoche …

  a very much wanted to be in *Jurassic Park*?
  b didn't want to be in *Jurassic Park*?
  c really wanted to play a dinosaur in *Jurassic Park*?

2 According to the writer, Gerard Depardieu's most popular films …

  a have been made in Hollywood.
  b have only been seen in Europe.
  c have been made in France, but seen in other countries, too.

3 The author mentions Brad Pitt, Jim Jarmusch and Elvis Presley to show that García Bernal …

  a has been accepted in an American context.
  b has worked with important American film people.
  c knows a lot about American music.

4 How does the writer feel about Javier Bardem's acting career in Hollywood?

    a He is uncertain Bardem will succeed.

    b He is confident Bardem will have a variety of roles.

    c He is worried that the public is more interested in Bardem's personal life.

5 What does the writer say about one foreign action hero?

    a Producers are reluctant to hire him.

    b He is less successful than other foreign actors.

    c A background in martial arts has been helpful to him.

6 The writer's purpose in writing this article is to suggest that …

    a American actors are able to earn more money than foreign actors.

    b a successful career in Europe or Latin America doesn't guarantee success in the United States.

    c Foreign actors generally do well in the United States.

COMPREHENSION 2   **Answer the questions.**

1 What is *the pond* in line 14?

    a the Atlantic Ocean

    b a different language

    c The United States

2 What is another way of saying *others shredded both the film and Depardieu's performance*? (line 21)

    … others thought Depardieu's performance and the film were …

    a complex

    b interesting

    c terrible

3 In line 26, when the writer says *hometown hero* does he mean that Brad Pitt is …

    a popular with ordinary Americans?

    b very famous in the place he was born?

    c uncomfortable when working in large cities?

4 From the different parts of the word, what do you think *monosyllabic* (line 40) means?

    a having one idea in mind

    b speaking in words of one syllable

    c with one partner

5 In line 45, what does *an item* mean?

   a part of a group

   b boyfriend and girlfriend

   c recently divorced

6 Use your own words to rewrite *Maybe the one genre where foreign actors have an edge is in action films* (line 48)

Action film is one genre where foreign actors _____

7 In line 50, the expression *a solid grounding in* refers to …

   a the place where Van Damme did his kick boxing.

   b a particular style of kick boxing.

   c Van Damme's extensive experience of kick boxing.

8 In line 59, the writer chooses the verb *heading* for reasons of style. This is because …

   a the first sound, /h/, is the same as the first sound in Hollywood.

   b *heading* is a formal word.

   c it is a way of avoiding repetition.

VOCABULARY SKILLS

Use a dictionary to find the meaning of the following words from the text. Then choose the correct words to complete the sentences.

1 *success (n)* (line 11) ———————————————

They did their best to *have / achieve / make* a success *in / of / with* their business.

2 *nominated (v)* (line 29) ———————————————

She was nominated *for / to / by* the Oscar *for / to / by* the Academy.

3 *imagination (n)* (line 38) ———————————————

It's important to *evolve / tease / stimulate* a child's imagination.

4 *fascinated (adj)* (line 51) ———————————————

We were all fascinated *with / by / about* her latest film.

GRAMMAR 1

Read the examples from the text and answer the questions.

1 *She'd be happy to be in* Jurassic Park **as long as** *she could play a dinosaur.* (lines 3-4) is a conditional structure.

   a Which word could we substitute for *as long as*?

   b Which of the two options makes the condition seem more important?

2 *One possible exception was* Green Card ... *where **he plays** a French immigrant* (lines 16–17)

Why is the present simple used?

a to describe a habit or routine

b to describe actions in films, plays and books

3 *The problem for Bardem is **that he now needs a really big hit to consolidate his success so far**.* (lines 45-47)

The *that* clause in bold is a complement of *be* in this example and works with *the problem*. Which of the examples below is incorrect?

a The truth is that I hate him.

b The difficulty is that she is very good at her job.

c The month of December is that it is a very difficult time of the year.

4 1) *every now and again a foreign actor will capture the imagination* (lines 37-38)

2) *a whole generation of people will remember him* (lines 57-58)

In these sentences, *will* is used in different ways. Which sentence talks about a continuous action and which talks about a repeated action?

GRAMMAR 2 **You are going to interview a famous film director. Complete the questions.**

1 How long _____ you _____(make) films?

2 What kind of films _____ you _____(enjoy) watching as a child?

3 What _____(make) you decide to become a director?

4 Who are the most interesting actors that you _____(direct)?

5 _____ you ever _____(be) surprised at the reviews of your films?

6 What _____(be) the worst thing that ever _____(happen) during the making of one of your films?

SPEAKING **Take turns with a partner to be the interviewer and director in Grammar 2. Use your imagination when you answer the questions!**

Effective • *Skills*

ACTIVATING KNOWLEDGE 1

Read the dialogue below. Find out ...

a whether Emma enjoyed the film or not.

b the reason for her reaction.

Christine: So, what did you think of it?

Emma: It was a bit of a let-down, actually.

Christine: Why's that?

Emma: Well, it was full of clichés.

Christine: Such as?

Emma: The way they meet, for example. He bumps into her, she drops her papers, and he picks them up! That's so unoriginal! And when she sees him in a restaurant with another woman, but it's really his sister!

Christine: Well, OK, but it was entertaining!

ACTIVATING KNOWLEDGE 2

Think about the clichés in films that you have seen. Complete the sentences in the table (*Your guess*).

	Your guess	Website comments
When a man and a woman bump into each other, she always drops	*her papers.*	
Cars that crash must always		1
When people speak on the phone, they never		2
Police bosses are always angry with		3
When the heroine gets into her car (when the villain is chasing her), she		4
In martial arts films, the hero wants to get revenge for the death of		5
Whenever someone wakes up from a nightmare they		6

SCANNING   **Read the emails that were sent to the Film Reviewer's Guide website. Complete the website comments in Activating knowledge 2 with the clichés the writers describe.**

Did you think of the same clichés as the website authors?

MOVIE REVIEWER'S GUIDE
The clichés you love to hate

A

I personally love action films, but clearly some are far better than others. What's the most unoriginal plot that comes up again and again? In my opinion, it has to be the police officer who does things his own way. His boss is always shouting at him and, about ten minutes into the film, he suspends him from duty (after he's destroyed yet another police car by driving it through a mall in pursuit of some crooks). He has to hand over his badge and his gun, but, of course, he continues to hunt down the crooks. And guess what – at the end of the film he's badly wounded, but still manages to shoot every crook and save a beautiful woman! Do we ever, ever need to see that again?
author: h_williams5

B

This one has to be the worst! Someone's having a nightmare – sometimes you can see what they're seeing, but it's kind of blurry – and when they wake they sit up! Sometimes there's a bit of panting and sweating, too, but they always have to sit bolt upright. I mean, come on! If I have a nightmare, I just lie in the dark and wonder why my husband has to snore so loud!
author: jenny_370

C

I can't believe how many times I've seen this happen in a film – big car chase, hero and villain doing impossible stunts at incredible speeds, suddenly a car crashes and straight away explodes in flames. I mean, when have you ever heard of this happening in real life? And if the car doesn't blow up immediately, it's guaranteed that it will as soon as the main stars have run far enough away from the wreck. Talk about unoriginal!
author: trashman

D

In those films where the hero is an expert in martial arts, it's also necessary that he's poor, but honest. He only uses his skills when he's absolutely pushed to the limit, so the plot of the film usually requires him to seek revenge for the murder of his girlfriend (poor, but
30 honest), a family member, or his elderly master. On the way, various crooks try to tempt him into a life of crime, but he remains pure. Oh, and his fights have to involve a series of opponents, each more evil and powerful than the last. In the final showdown, despite all sorts of pain from bullets or broken bones, he wins. Sometimes I think a child
35 could write the scripts for these films – they're all the same!
author: mikelau83

E

Phone conversations in films are very odd. Do you ever notice how characters don't identify themselves when they answer the phone? Especially in police films, phone conversations are bizarre – really brief and abrupt. No time for a 'thanks' or 'see you' at the end, either. How are these guys supposed to solve any crimes
40 at all when they have the communication skills of monkeys? Weird.
author: theenigma

F

It makes me laugh when you see the heroine running in high heels. Why doesn't she just take her shoes off? When she finally makes it to her car, she can't get the keys in the ignition because
45 she's so nervous. Of course, she starts the car in the nick of time and she gets away, but not before the crazy psycho guy has smashed in the window with an axe!
author: kittycool1

UNDERSTANDING ATTITUDE AND OPINION

Read the emails again and answer the questions.

1 In A, how does the boss punish the police officer?

2 What has the police officer done to deserve this punishment?

3 Why is it surprising that the police officer finally kills all his enemies?

4 Which phrasal verb in B shows the writer's attitude of disbelief?

5 Why does the writer in C disapprove of scenes in which cars explode?

6 Which phrase in D tells us that the martial arts hero must be under a lot of pressure before he uses his skills?

7 How would you describe the writer's attitude in the final sentence in E?

   a surprised   **b** anxious   **c** sarcastic

8 In F, what do you understand by *in the nick of time*?

VOCABULARY EXTENSION

What do these expressions mean?

1 *to hand over*

    a to hide   **b** to give/offer   **c** to search/find

2 *to hunt down*

    a to find every member of a group   **b** to run and escape from people
    c to kill people one by one

3 *(it's) guaranteed (that)*

    a often   **b** almost certain   **c** sure

4 *talk about (+ adj)*

    the writer is ...

    a inviting other people to comment   **b** emphasizing his opinion
    c criticizing the dialogue

5 *In the final showdown*

    a just before everyone dies   **b** in the last fight scene
    c at the very end of the film

6 *to smash in (glass)*

    a to make a hole   **b** to attack   **c** to break into pieces

DISCUSSION

You are planning the story for a really clichéd romance. Discuss the following points:

1 Who are the main characters (personal details/appearance/occupation, etc.)?

2 How do the main characters meet or get to know each other?

3 Where is the film set? (time and location)

4 What is the basic story for the beginning, middle, and end of the film?

5 Where does the final scene take place and what do the characters say?

WRITING

Complete the text below about a film cliché. Choose either:

a a film about teenagers going to a haunted house

b a film about a tough guy who has to rescue someone

Every time I see a film about _____, it's always full of the same clichés. It's guaranteed that _____ and (they/he/one of them) always has to _____. Of course, (there/they/he) _____. And, guess what? At the end of the film (there/they/he) _____. Talk about _____!

Read the text.

Super Size Me

In 2004, American independent film-maker Morgan Spurlock released *Super Size Me*, a feature-length documentary that attacked the fast-food industry and specifically McDonald's. The title comes from McDonald's former policy of encouraging customers to buy the largest size of whatever they ordered from the menu, which Spurlock regarded as one of the factors contributing to the obesity epidemic in children and adults sweeping the United States.

The documentary largely took the form of an experiment in which Spurlock aimed to eat only McDonald's food three times a day for thirty days. At the outset of the film, he weighed a healthy 185.51 pounds, but gained 24.5 pounds by the end of the month. During this time, he experienced mood swings, sexual dysfunction, and severe liver damage, to the extent that his doctor insisted he return to a normal diet immediately. Spurlock also suffered depression, lethargy and headaches, and found to his horror that these could be relieved by eating more McDonald's food. In other words, he had become addicted to its high sugar and casein content.

The film was nominated for an Academy Award and was one of the highest-earning documentaries in the US that year. The McDonald's Corporation, however, was not amused and set up a website (www.supersizeme-thedebate.co.uk) to dispute Spurlock's claims. At the same time, it also discontinued its Super Size policy, but denied it had anything to do with the film.

EXERCISE 2

Answer the questions as quickly possible.

1   Morgan Spurlock called his film *Super Size Me* as a reference to ...

   a   the fact that he had enjoyed fast food meals since childhood.

   b   the way that McDonald's persuaded people to buy large portions.

   c   the trend in the US for people to be overweight.

2   The effects of just eating fast food led Morgan Spurlock to experience ...

   a   certain psychological problems.

   b   a change in attitude towards the fast food industry.

   c   doubts about continuing the experiment.

3   According to the writer, what happened after the film was released?

   a   Morgan Spurlock acknowledged that parts of his film were misleading.

   b   The McDonald's Corporation was forced to admit that its Super Size policy was wrong.

   c   US cinemas sold a large number of tickets for *Super Size Me*.

EXERCISE 1

Read the text.

Film

When was the last time you came out of a **very successful** film and really felt you'd got your money's worth? It's hard not to be disappointed nowadays, since every film receives huge amounts of publicity months before it's released, and inevitably it won't live up to your expectations. Even Hollywood seems to have realized that its best film-making years are over, which is possibly the reason why we seem to be faced with so many remakes recently.

If you're a **fan of film**, you'll know that *King Kong* was originally released in 1933, again in 1976, and once more in 2005. The **main female actor puts on a good show**, and the big gorilla looks more realistic, but isn't a third form of this story a little excessive? *War of the Worlds* first terrified audiences in 1953; the budget wouldn't even have covered Tom Cruise's salary in his adaptation last year. The latest remake falls into the thriller-mystery **type of film**, with Nicolas Cage as the star in *The Wicker Man*. The location moves from Scotland to somewhere off the Washington coast, and audiences who are too young to remember the 1973 film will still be gripped by the **suspense**. Nevertheless, **professional opinion** is that surely there are other stories worthy of the big screen? When you remake a classic, it is **easy to guess** the result will always be a poor imitation.

EXERCISE 2

Answer the questions.

1 What can we infer about the writer's attitude to remade films?

   a He believes in general that they are not worth doing.

   b He feels that some are better adaptations than others.

   c He thinks that remakes require well-known actors to be successful.

2 Replace the words/phrases in **bold** in the text with words from the texts in Unit 4. The first letter of each word is given as a clue.

   a h_____   d the l_____

   b p_____   e r_____

   c g_____   f p_____

5 • Fashion

PRE-READING 1 **Complete the sentences with the words in the box.**

| exotic location   supermodel   a catwalk   cosmetics   reality TV shows |

1 Who is your favourite _____, and why?

2 Why are so many people keen to appear on
   _____?

3 If you could choose any _____ for a holiday, what
   would it be?

4 What do you think is most difficult for a model when she goes down
   a _____?

5 A lot of young men in the United States and Europe are starting to
   use _____. What do you think about this?

Discuss 1–5 above with a partner.

PRE-READING 2 **Find words 1–4 below in the text. Read the sentence(s) around
them. Match the words to the correct definitions (a–d) and write
the translations.**

1 ritual humiliation   _____

2 aspiring   _____

3 humanly possible   _____

4 couturier   _____

a wanting to be and working towards something that you are not now

b the experience of being regularly and continually made to feel stupid
   or embarrassed

c a person who designs clothes

d able to be done by a person

Next Top Model – globalization for TV!

'Congratulations, you are still in the running towards becoming *America's Next Top Model*'. Five points for guessing the name of the TV programme this quote comes from and ten points for knowing the name of the person who says it. Well, the answer to the first question is *America's Next Top Model* and the quote comes from the show's host, supermodel Ms Tyra Banks. If you got them both right, chances are you are part of a growing global community because the Next Top Model concept is rapidly spreading round the world.

There's nothing particularly new about this programme. Reality TV shows have been with us since the late 1940s. However, Tyra Banks has brought some glamour to the genre by setting the ritual humiliation that is part of any reality show in the context of the fashion industry.

There are plenty of opportunities for conflict as the aspiring models go through a variety of tasks all related to the day-to-day work of being a model. Every series also has its 'exotic location' episode where the entire cast and crew are flown off to another country, usually somewhere warm with nice beaches, to give the viewers a change of scene.

Of course the climax of every episode is when the judges, led by Tyra, discuss every contestant and decide which two have been the least successful this particular week. In the proud tradition of reality TV, this process is drawn out longer than one would think humanly possible, with Tyra starting with the most successful and solemnly repeating what all the contestants desperately want to hear: 'Congratulations, you are still in the running towards becoming America's next top model.' Finally she gets to the last two and their performances are picked over once more. Then, with more never-ending pauses and plenty of dramatic music, she puts the weakest contestant out of her misery and sends her home.

Obviously there are millions of viewers out there who are very interested in fashion, and using the reality TV format keeps them entertained. There is no doubt that within each episode the audience does catch a glimpse of the world of fashion and there is no shortage of beautiful clothes and beautiful people on display. However, not everybody is convinced. Karl Lagerfeld should know more than most about the fashion industry, as he has been one of the world's leading couturiers for the last 40 years – but he is less than impressed. '*America's Next Top Model* is trash that is funny for five minutes if you're with other people. If you're alone, it's not funny.'

Despite Karl's reservations, the rest of the world is only too keen to jump on the *Next Top Model* bandwagon. So far the idea has been picked up by nearly 40 countries. As one would expect, almost every European country has already screened it or is busily making its own version. Austria and Ireland joined in 2009 and Germany, Belgium and France have run the series for some time. But it is clearly not just a 'western' phenomenon, since other countries around the world are getting involved; and perhaps most surprising of all, there are even plans for a series entitled *Afghanistan's Next Top Model*.

No matter where the programmes are made it, seems that the attraction is generally the same. Of course the competition element keeps us tuning in to find out who will shine through, but people seem to be equally drawn to the fashion element. It is always interesting to check out what goes on behind the scenes in the glamorous world of fashion where we get a privileged glimpse of what designers are creating right now and what the people in this industry actually do day-to-day.

In one recent episode, the girls had to model clothes in the front window of a high-street shop. In another, their task was to stay upright on a winding catwalk while wearing 7-inch heels and very tight skirts. A common assignment is the cosmetics commercial. This is a good opportunity to see how the contestants perform under pressure. There is no shortage of hot lights and even hotter tempers. All of these challenges are part of a working model's day.

For the audience, escaping from our everyday lives and seeing worlds that are beyond our own experience is a major attraction. The 'exotic location' episode feeds into this but there are also the fantasies that this kind of TV can inspire in the viewers. While we are watching we can daydream about wearing fabulous clothes and being seen at exclusive international events. We can also relate to the stress that the contestants feel as they go through their various tasks and assignments. But sitting comfortably at home, we reckon that we would do far better if we were in their places. We can see the mistakes they make. Don't they realize that the judges are watching them and can hear every word they say?

Whatever the reason, it seems fairly clear that programmes like Next Top Model are here to stay. They obviously appeal to a wide range of viewers and of course they are relatively cheap to make. Are they great art? Well I guess that depends on your definition of 'great art', but as a pleasant way of spending a lazy half hour or so Next Top Model is probably not too damaging.

COMPREHENSION 1   **Answer the questions.**

1 The writer thinks that the fashion industry is …

   a difficult and embarrassing for models.

   b a good subject for reality TV.

2 The judges take a long time to make a decision because …

   a the contestants are very similar.

   b they want to make the programme more dramatic.

3 According to the writer, what is the main reason people like the programme?

   a They like fashion.

   b They like competitions.

4 In the last paragraph, the writer's opinion is that *Next Top Model* …

   a is high-quality TV.

   b is harmless entertainment.

COMPREHENSION 2   **Answer the questions.**

1 To be *in the running* (line 1) means that the contestant …

   a can return next week.

   b is out of the competition.

   c has won *Next Top Model*.

2 Usually the word *conflict* has a negative connotation but in line 14, the writer uses it in a positive way. This is because …

   a the models have to compete against each other.

   b the writer is being ironic.

   c the programme would be boring if all the contestants liked each other.

3 When Tyra Banks *puts the weakest contestant out of her misery* (lines 29-30) she is being kind to the contestant by …

   a giving her advice about her modelling.

   b allowing her to return next week.

   c finally making a decision.

4 In lines 38-39, what is meant by *less than impressed*?

Karl Lagerfeld …

   a is not a popular designer.

   b doesn't enjoy *Next Top Model*.

   c is still successful, despite his age.

5   *To jump on the bandwagon* (lines 41-42) means …

    a   to join something successful for your own benefit.

    b   to follow the lead of a powerful country, e.g. the United States.

    c   to take an idea and adapt it to your own country.

6   *Of course* (line 52) in English has a stronger meaning than the translation in other languages. What is the function of *of course* in this context?

    a   It shows agreement.

    b   It implies that something is obvious.

    c   It indicates that the speaker has changed their opinion.

7   In line 64, the writer uses the phrase *even hotter tempers* to imply that, in this section of the programme …

    a   the temperature in the room rises.

    b   the people involved get very angry.

    c   the models that succeed are very attractive.

8   In lines 77, what is the function of *whatever the reason?*

The writer …

    a   suggests that the success of the show is a bad thing.

    b   doesn't care why the show is successful.

    c   thinks that there are a number of reasons for the show's success.

VOCABULARY SKILLS 1   **Guess the definition of these phrasal verbs from the text. Find out whether the phrasal verb is transitive (T) or intransitive (I). Check your answers in a dictionary.**

Phrasal verb	Definition	T/I	Translation
go through (line 15)			
draw out (line 23)			
pick over (lines 28)			
pick up (line 43)			
shine through (line 53)			
check out (line 55)			

VOCABULARY SKILLS 2

Complete the sentences with the phrasal verbs from Vocabulary skills 1.

1 Why did he _____ every last detail before he made up his mind? We knew who he would choose hours ago.

2 The most interesting thing is that the models with real talent always _____ in the end.

3 Let's buy a paper. We can _____ what's on at the cinema.

4 I really hope one of the networks will _____ the show. I think it's a great idea.

5 It's important to _____ the early stages carefully. Otherwise you'll never be successful later.

6 I don't know why the judges had to _____ it _____ for so long. I thought they'd never finish.

Grammar

Gerunds

escaping from our everyday lives and **seeing** worlds that are beyond our own experience is a major attraction.

The words in **bold** above are gerunds. They act as nouns – in this case referring to the general idea of escaping from a job and seeing different worlds.

GRAMMAR

Complete the sentences with gerunds. Use the words in the box in the correct form.

pose	day-dream	work	wear	diet	keep	wear

1 _____ up with the latest trends is important to many TV producers.

2 _____ make-up was forbidden when I was at school.

3 _____ reality TV shows is something most people enjoy.

4 _____ for a top fashion house is my dream!

5 _____ for photographs is second nature to successful models.

6 Constant _____ is bad for your health.

7 If you live in a cold country, _____ about beaches and sunshine is only natural.

8 _____ to walk in very high heels is usually very important for a model.

SPEAKING

Discuss the questions with a partner.

1 How interested are you in fashion?

2 What would you wear in the following situations:
going out with friends on Sunday;
going to a club or a party;
going to a job interview?

How interested are you in fashion?

Effective • *Skills*

ACTIVATING
KNOWLEDGE **You are going to read a text on the subject of foot binding in China. First choose the correct description of foot binding.**

a   Wrapping a woman's feet in cloth to stop them growing

b   A method of preventing servants or slaves from running away

c   A way of treating people for illness by massaging points on the feet

Read the questions below and guess the answers. Discuss your answers with a partner.

1   When did the practice of foot binding start? (_____ years ago)

2   Which social classes did foot binding affect?

3   What were some of the health problems caused by foot binding?

4   Who performed the procedure of foot binding?

5   How many women probably had their feet bound?

6   When did the practice of foot binding come to an end?

INFERRING **What is the meaning of the words in bold? Match the words to a definition (a–h).**

1   There are a number of **legends** concerning the **origins** of foot binding.

2   These women … became **confined** to their home.

3   This left them powerless and **subservient** to their husbands.

4   The cold would **numb** the pain.

5   Unbound feet meant shame and therefore social **exclusion**.

6   We can only begin to imagine the suffering that (these women) and their female **ancestors** had to **endure**.

a   When someone is deliberately prevented from being part of something

b   An old story about past events and famous people, usually untrue

c   The place or moment when something begins to exist

d   Someone who is related to you who lived a long time ago

e   To suffer something difficult in a patient way over a long period

f   To make someone stays in a place because they are too ill, weak, or disabled to leave

g   To make a part of your body lose its ability to feel

h   Considered less important and therefore obedient

a thousand years of *foot binding*

There are a number of **legends** concerning the **origins** of foot binding, but it seems likely that it started as a fashion among court dancers of the T'ang Dynasty (A.D. 618–690). It then became a required procedure for all royal females, and then girls of wealthy
5 families. These women inevitably became **confined** to their home and were dependent on personal servants for their every need. This left them powerless and **subservient** to their husbands and other males in their family – which was part of Confucian thinking. What may have started out as a fashion for small feet quickly became a
10 symbol of social status. In other words, bound feet were necessary to protect the honour of a family. While we may feel great sympathy for these upper-class women, the situation of women of lower classes who were expected to continue with heavy labour at home and in the fields must have been far worse. And as the practice
15 spread throughout the general population of China and lasted for nearly one thousand years, it is estimated that nearly a billion women endured the suffering it inflicted.

There were variations in the procedure itself, but the following provides a general overview. Between the ages of four and seven,
20 usually during winter time, when the cold would **numb** the pain, a girl's four small toes were broken and forced under the sole of her foot. A bandage was tightly wrapped around the toes, keeping them in place. It was further tightened each day and this continued for at least another two years until the girl's feet were virtually useless. In
25 addition to being subjected to this pain, a woman with bound feet would be at risk of infection if her toenails cut into her foot. The lack of circulation could also result in gangrene, so the foot had to be massaged daily to get the blood moving. Pus and blood had to be washed away every day as the smell was highly offensive. However,
30 women's bound feet could also be the subject of erotic poetry and many considered that no woman could be seen as sexually desirable without them.

When the time came, it would be a girl's own mother who broke her toes and bound her feet. This may seem to us inexplicably cruel, but
35 we have to consider that this was the only way to ensure a daughter could get married, no matter whether she was from a rich or poor

family. Unbound feet meant shame and therefore social **exclusion** for her family.

40 There was a weak attempt during the Qing Dynasty to put an end to foot binding, but tradition could not be defeated. The next attempt was nearly 270 years later when Sun Yat-Sen declared the practice to be illegal in the 1911 revolution. But it was not until the Anti-Foot Binding Movement in the 1920s that the practice finally and quickly came to an end. How 45 did members of the movement convince the vast population of China to turn so rapidly against a thousand-year-old tradition? Primarily, they pointed out how the rest of the world was laughing at this cruel and primitive custom, unique to China. They protested that weak women could only produce weak boys. They said that women could 50 not share equal status or be as useful with their feet bound, so at last this practice came to an end. It is still possible to find old women with tiny broken feet in parts of China and Taiwan. We can only begin to imagine the suffering that they and their female **ancestors** had to **endure.**

SCANNING **Read the text as quickly as possible and find the answers to Activating Knowledge.**

ANALYZING **Decide if the information about the text is True (T), False (F),**
MEANING **or Not Given (NG). Write T, F, or NG.**

1 The court dancers were chosen for their naturally small feet. ☐

2 Women from wealthy families had their feet bound to protect their family's reputation. ☐

3 By working in the fields, a woman could escape the foot binding procedure. ☐

4 An identical method for binding a girl's foot was practised all over China. ☐

5 Only women with bound feet were considered to be attractive. ☐

6 Members of the Anti-Foot Binding Movement regarded women as having the same intellectual ability as men. ☐

RECOGNIZING KEY WORDS AND MAIN IDEAS

Complete the summary with words from the text.

The process of foot binding usually took (**1**) *three years* or more to complete. The toes were first broken in (**2**)_____, so that the pain was less severe. After this, the girl's toes were forced under her feet and kept there with a (**3**)_____. There were a number of possible health risks that foot binding could cause, for example (**4**)_____ could occur if a woman's toenails cut her foot, and if blood could not flow properly. There was also a chance of (**5**)_____, which is why the foot required constant massage.

DISCUSSION

Discuss the questions with a partner.

1   What is the most surprising thing for you about foot binding?

2   Do we have the right to criticize the traditions of other countries?

3   What other fashions have restricted women's freedom? Do you think men are restricted by fashion?

WRITING

Read the extracts from an essay below. Use a–d to complete the sentences and the words in bold to help you.

Young people today are too interested in fashion and this makes them superficial.

The question whether an interest in fashion makes a person shallow or not **depends on** (**1**)___c___. We have to consider how much time and money is devoted to keeping up with the latest trends, **compared to** (**2**)_____.

Young people who are obsessed with fashion are often willing to wear whatever high-fashion stores are selling. Furthermore, they do not consider **whether** (**3**)_____, and they are prepared to pay a high price. What is most important to them is their image. They want other people, **especially** (**4**)_____, to be impressed by the labels they are wearing.

a   what is spent on other pastimes or activities

b   their peer group

c   the *extent* of the interest

d   the outfit they buy is flattering or not

Now write paragraph 3 in defence of young people. Give reasons why they are not superficial. Then write a concluding paragraph.

6 • Controversy!

PRE-READING 1 **Which of the following things are most important to you? Rank them from 1 (most important) to 5 (least important).**

> your religion   your country   art   your privacy
> how other people spend their money

PRE-READING 2 **Find the words in bold in the text and then choose the correct answer, a or b.**

1   Scientists use **formaldehyde** to …

   a   stop dead animals from rotting.

   b   take the skin off dead animals.

2   The **general public** describes …

   a   people who go to art galleries.

   b   ordinary men and women.

3   A **taxidermist** shop usually …

   a   arranges funerals.

   b   sells stuffed animals or fish.

4   **Human remain**s are …

   a   the things people leave to their relatives after they die.

   b   what's left of a person's body after they die.

5   **Common decency** means …

   a   behaving in a way that most people in your society or social group expect and believe to be honest and moral.

   b   doing what you believe to be right even if other people in your society or social group disagree with you.

I love it! I hate it!

'Why on earth would anyone want to put a dead shark in a glass case?' … 'Euugh, that's disgusting! Her dirty clothes? Yuck!' … 'How insulting! He's calling our country a toilet!' These comments and more like them are heard every day in art galleries around the world. If you want controversy, where better to look than in an art gallery?

But why? Damien Hirst, Tracey Emin and David Cerny are all extremely successful contemporary artists. It is their work that elicited these shocked responses. Hirst's enormous shark preserved in **formaldehyde**, displayed at The Metropolitan Museum of Modern Art in New York, Emin's obviously slept-in bed, surrounded by her filthy clothes and exhibited at The Tate Gallery in London, and Cerny's mosaic, which represents the countries of the European Union at the European Council Building in Brussels, all trigger very strong emotions but for quite different reasons.

20 Hirst seems to upset people because he challenges the very idea of what art is. For those members of the **general public** whose idea of art is a painting by a traditional artist like Rembrandt, then a stuffed shark is not going to get a favourable response, and typically leads to comments like: 'Well, that's not art. Anyone could do it.' Tracey Emin, on the other hand, seems intent on offending her audience by putting her personal life on display. This provokes debate over what's taboo and what's not and enrages people who would rather not see the workings of the human body exhibited. And of course, Cerny

25 takes us into cultural and political controversy with his EU mosaic. He depicts France as a country always on strike, Romania as a Dracula theme park and Germany as a network of motorways vaguely resembling a swastika. And in this way, he pokes fun at national identity, offending many countries along the way.

30 A later piece by Damien Hirst that has created a different kind of controversy is his diamond skull. He bought a genuine skull from a **taxidermist** shop in London and made a plastic replica, which he encrusted with high-quality diamonds. He then fixed the teeth from the original skull into his artwork and called it *For The Love Of God*.

35 He used 8,601 diamonds and the sculpture cost £14 million to make. With this piece, he could potentially be offending people on several levels. Firstly, some cultures view **human remains** as sacred and think they should be treated with great respect, but Hirst creates a bizarre ornament out of a skull. Then, by putting God into the title

40 he runs the risk of offending the Church. Finally, there is the cost factor. £14 million could pay for countless blankets for the homeless or help hundreds of poor children to learn to read. How is it possible that Hirst could waste so much money on a 'work of art'?

Human beings are good at being shocked and outraged. Art seems to

45 touch a raw nerve. Our religious beliefs, our sense of **common decency**, our self image or simply how we think other people's money should be spent, are all major issues that are close to our hearts. That is why we have such strong opinions about them. Perhaps this is also why the Hirsts, Emins and Cernys of this world

50 choose these topics to base their work upon. Hirst said that his skull 'celebrates death'. He is dealing with important issues and challenging preconceived ways of thinking about the world. If our artists only dealt with what is safe and unimportant, what use would they be?

COMRPEHENSION 1 **Read the text and answer the question.**

The writer's main point in this article is …

a To explain why people don't like modern art.

b To encourage people to think more about their own reaction to modern art.

c To criticize the amount of money that is wasted on modern art.

COMPREHENSION 2 **Match the sentence halves to make logical statements. Use the information in the text to help you. <u>Underline</u> the part of the text where you find the information.**

1 Art galleries are a good place

2 Hirst's, Emin's and Cerny's work often causes people

3 Many people believe it should be difficult

4 Depicting EU countries using national stereotypes

5 Some artists do not respect

6 The money involved in creating Hirst's skull could have been used

7 People are skilled when it comes

8 An artist's job is to challenge people

a caused considerable offence.

b to being offended and upset.

c to reflect on important issues.

d to create art.

e society's taboos.

f to react strongly.

g to find controversy.

h to improve people's lives.

COMPREHENSION 3 **Answer the questions.**

1 In line 8, what is meant by *contemporary artists*?

Artists who are …

a working now.

b popular now.

c retired now.

2 In line 14, what does *all* refer to?

3 In line 14, which phrase means *to cause people to have strong feelings*?

4 In line 28, what is another way of saying *vaguely resembling*?

a looking a bit like.

b being exactly the same as.

c trying to be different from.

5 In line 33, what does *encrusted* mean?

   a to protect

   b to make very beautiful

   c to cover with something hard

6 In line 49, who does the phrase *the Hirsts, Emins and Cernys of this world* refer to?

VOCABULARY SKILLS

Find words in the text that match the definitions.

1 A very strong feeling of dislike that almost makes you sick (*adj*) (lines 1-2)

2 A group of different things that are arranged together (*n*) (lines 13-14)

3 To make somebody extremely angry (*v*) (lines 22-24)

4 To show someone or something in a picture (*v*) (lines 26-28)

5 An exact copy of something (*n*) (lines 31-33)

6 Something that is beautiful rather than useful (*n*) (lines 37-39)

7 With the possibility of (*adv*) (lines 40-43)

8 Ideas or opinions formed before you have enough knowledge or experience (*adj*) (lines 50-54)

Grammar	If our artists only **dealt** with what is safe and unimportant, what use **would** they **be**?
Second conditional	This is an example of the second conditional. The second conditional is used to talk about an unreal situation in the present or future. In other words we are **imagining** a situation where artists dealt with safe and unimportant things.

GRAMMAR **Write sentences with the following prompts. Decide …**

- which clause should use a past form.
- which clause should use *would/could* + infinitive.
- where *if* should go.
- where the comma should go.

For example:

I / be / an artist / I / paint / portraits

If I was an artist, I would paint portraits.

1 more people / study / art / they / like / it more

_____

2 Damien Hirst / spend / less money / he / not offend / people so much

_____

3 more people / think / about art / the world / be / a better place

_____

4 you / be / rich / you / buy / expensive art ?

_____

5 artists / not shock / people / they / not be / famous

_____

6 I / not like / art / I / not go / to galleries

_____

7 people / not be / so emotional about art / they / understand / it better

_____

8 we / not care / about art / we / not be / offended by it

_____

Effective • *Skills*

ACTIVATING
VOCABULARY **You are going to read an interview with a graffiti artist. First use your dictionary to translate these words. Which six words do you think are in the interview?**

1   a spray can   _____

2   risk (*n*)   _____

3   a sketch   _____

4   a design   _____

5   a portrait   _____

6   a paint brush   _____

7   destruction (*n*)   _____

8   a ghetto   _____

9   a tag   _____

10   a gallery   _____

PREDICTING **During the interview, the artist mentions the following things. What do you think he says about them?**

1   *cartoons*

    a   I drew these before graffiti art.

    b   Graffiti art and cartoons can share the same humour.

    c   Graffiti is more political than cartoons.

2   *the police*

    a   The police have a policy of tolerance towards most graffiti.

    b   The police don't allow us any freedom.

    c   Some police officers appreciate what we are trying to express.

3   *gangs*

    a   Different gangs of artists have different styles.

    b   Many gang members just spray tags, not paintings.

    c   There is a lot of competition between the gangs.

SCANNING 1 **Read what the artist says to review your answers to Activating vocabulary and Predicting. <u>Underline</u> the parts of the text that give you the answers.**

IS IT ART?

A I'm a graffiti artist who goes out and paints in the streets during the night, when most civilized people are sleeping, but also during the day on legal walls or 'free walls' as they're called in Switzerland. Mostly these walls are in old factories, youth clubs, or some such place. All I use is an idea, a sketchbook, and a spray can.

B Sure, but like most graffiti artists, I have the attitude 'no risk, no fun.' If the police catch you, it will cost you a fortune to have the walls cleaned. Most sprayers always spray the same tag, so it can be recognized and they can become famous, but if the police catch you in the act, this also gives them the evidence that it was you who was responsible for all the other tagging. Fines in this case could easily cost you thousands of dollars. That's why certain famous graffiti artists who had problems with the police had to leave the country.

C Graffiti is a style of art which was invented during the 1980s in the United States by the kids who lived in the ghettos. Through graffiti they could express their feelings and their anger. But that's just one part of it. Most of it is just fun, and it's about competition between different artists and gangs. It's a way of fighting with each other without using guns and fists. It's the same thing with rap, human beat box, dee jaying, and break dancing – the other four elements of hip hop – it's all about competition to see who's the greatest.

D Yes, but not commercially driven ones. This kind of art is real and honest because you'll never earn money with it, so it's all just for the scene and for yourself, which is what art should be. What I want to do with my art is to bring colour to the gray areas of the city where there are no plants or trees, or other real signs of life. I want to show other people that another more vibrant world is possible, and that they just have to wake up and realize that they don't have to live in a sterile environment. What I also hope is that one day, even the older generation will like my paintings and understand what they're saying.

E I often ask myself if what I do is OK because it causes damage and that's not something you can overlook. But I made rules for myself, like to respect old houses, brick walls, and people's cars. I just spray on gray concrete walls or on walls which are already full of tags. I don't wanna annoy other people, but sometimes there's no way to avoid it.

F I had always painted cartoons or naturalistic stuff since I was about five, but one day a guy joined our class who was a member of a famous crew. He always did his graffiti sketches during lessons, and I thought they were pretty impressive, so I wanted to learn that style as well. At the beginning, he always said that I was a 'toy' – that's a bad graffiti artist – till another friend showed me the rules for graffiti painting. For me, graffiti is the attempt to harmonize shape and colour. You want to make every single thing perfect, which is nearly impossible. So it's a never-ending quest to perfect your art. I'm sure that I'll never get to the point where I'm fed up with it.

G Certainly most people don't even see this as art because they're just not open-minded or receptive enough for it. They're too stressed to bother considering what it might mean and just see it as destruction. Actually, I think age is irrelevant. Before I was into graffiti myself, I never got what it was all about. Now I know nearly every important street artist by his artistic name.

H Sure, but it doesn't always go the way you planned. If you attempt to create something special it attracts more people, but now you're often forced to spray huge, ugly, black–silver graffs because you never know how long you've got! You need eyes in the back of your head to see if anyone is using a mobile phone to report you to the police. I'd say it's a pity we can't always create something beautiful, but we live in a repressive society.

SCANNING 2 **Match the interviewer's questions (1–8) to a paragraph in the interview (A–H).**

1 Do you think that your work has a wide appeal or is it just appreciated by young people?

2 Do you ever worry about getting into trouble?

3 How did you get into graffiti in the first place?

4 Do you consider that your art is harmful in any way?

5 Can you tell us something about the origins of graffiti?

6 Do you have any ideas for your next sketch?

7 Do you have any ambitions regarding your work?

8 When and where do you usually do your work?

DISCUSSION

Discuss this statement with a partner.

'Some people believe that graffiti is a crime and that the people who do it have no consideration for others. Others consider graffiti is a form of art and it should be encouraged.'

WRITING

You recently read an article about graffiti in an online English-language magazine. Part of the article appears below.

> For many commuters, all they can see outside the train window is endless tagging over the nearby buildings. It's difficult to understand why the offenders, mainly teenagers, feel the need to vandalize other people's property. Is imprisonment the answer?

You also read a reply from another reader. Complete and improve the following email with the adverbs in the box. Sometimes more than one answer is possible.

constantly	greatly	absolutely	certainly
personally	probably	terribly	incredibly

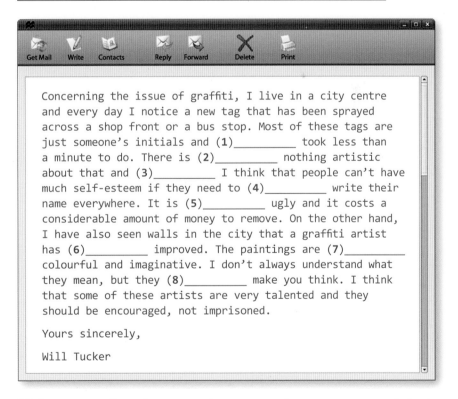

Concerning the issue of graffiti, I live in a city centre and every day I notice a new tag that has been sprayed across a shop front or a bus stop. Most of these tags are just someone's initials and (1)_____ took less than a minute to do. There is (2)_____ nothing artistic about that and (3)_____ I think that people can't have much self-esteem if they need to (4)_____ write their name everywhere. It is (5)_____ ugly and it costs a considerable amount of money to remove. On the other hand, I have also seen walls in the city that a graffiti artist has (6)_____ improved. The paintings are (7)_____ colourful and imaginative. I don't always understand what they mean, but they (8)_____ make you think. I think that some of these artists are very talented and they should be encouraged, not imprisoned.

Yours sincerely,

Will Tucker

Write an email to the magazine expressing your own point of view.

EXERCISE 1

Read the text.

Fashion

Forget face lifts, breast implants, and Botox injections – the latest trend in New York City is cosmetic toe amputation* surgery. A growing number of New York women are opting for an operation that means they can squeeze their feet into pointy high-heeled shoes, preferably those made by designers Manolo Blahnik or Jimmy Choo. Advocates of the procedure stress the value of height in making the right impression in business and society circles. 'They give a woman that extra confidence in her appearance,' says New York podiatrist* Dr Fay Miller, who claims to have performed more than fifty 'foot enhancement surgeries.' In fact, the term 'amputation' has misled many would-be patients. The second toe is cut open, part of the bone is removed, and the toe is sewn back up, causing the flesh to shrink. This still seems gruesome, but is not actually whole amputation. Some members of the American Orthopedic Foot and Ankle Society deeply oppose this kind of operation, believing it can often result in permanent disability and be excruciating. They would also discourage women from wearing high heels since they can lead to a number of serious problems including knee, pelvic, back, and shoulder pain. Despite their warnings, New York women are continuing to make appointments with Dr Miller. Vanity, it seems, is a strong kind of painkiller.

*amputation = *the removal of a part of the body (for example an arm) in a medical operation*

*podiatrist = *a specialist in the care of feet and the treatment of foot diseases*

EXERCISE 2

Answer the questions.

1   According to the writer, why are women having operations on their feet?

   a   Their toes had been damaged as a result of wearing high heels.

   b   Other operations to improve their appearance have not satisfied them.

   c   Their feet do not fit the kind of shoe they want to wear.

2   What does the writer claim is confusing about this kind of foot surgery?

   a   What the operation involves.

   b   Who is legally allowed to perform it.

   c   The kind of physical problems it may cause.

3   Find a word in the text that means ...

   a   someone who strongly supports something.

   b   to make someone believe something that is incorrect.

   c   horrible/disgusting.

   d   to disagree with or disapprove of something.

   e   extremely painful.

   f   the fact of being too interested in your appearance.

EXERCISE 1

Read paragraphs
A and B.

Controversial issues

A   At 62, Patricia Rashbrook is so far the oldest woman in Britain to give birth. The healthy baby boy, nicknamed JJ, was conceived through IVF,* after several previously failed attempts. The treatment was carried out by Dr Antinori, an Italian doctor who runs a fertility clinic in Rome. The birth sparked controversy among those in the fertility profession and attracted media attention around the world. JJ was Ms Rashbrook's fourth child; the youngest of the other three was 18 when his new sibling was born. John Farrant, Ms Rashbrook's new husband, told the media that they were well able to meet the child's needs. The couple say that they are in good health, but in the event that they both meet an untimely death, friends have agreed to become surrogate parents.

B   We can divide opinion on this issue into two major camps. Those who are vehemently against older people giving birth say that the parents are only thinking of themselves. They believe that the child will be ashamed of having much older parents as he or she grows up. Furthermore, there is considerable likelihood that the child will be bereaved much sooner in life than is normal. Those in the other camp, however, point to the fact that many children are brought up by grandparents and benefit from this arrangement. Older parents can often offer the child greater financial security and constant devotion. Moreover, they argue that if the government ever started to impose legal restrictions on the types of people who could have children, there is no telling where those restrictions would end.

*IVF = In Vitro Fertilization: *the medical process in which a woman's egg is fertilized outside the body and then put back inside to grow into a baby*

EXERCISE 2

Paragraph A

Decide if the sentences are True (T), False (F), or if the information is Not Given (NG) in the text.

1   Ms Rashbrook became pregnant after one treatment of IVF. ☐

2   Dr Antinori treated Ms Rashbrook in his clinic. ☐

3   Ms Rashbrook wanted a child because her other children had left home. ☐

4   Ms Rashbrook and her husband believe they will have a long life. ☐

5   Ms Rashbrook and her husband have not decided what will happen to the child if they die. ☐

Paragraph B

1   Which three reasons are given against older people having children?

   a   the child's embarrassment

   b   the child's potential health problems

   c   the early death of the child's parents

   d   the lack of energy the parents have

   e   the money problems older people face

   f   the selfishness of the parents

2   What point is being made in the final sentence?

   a   It is difficult to say what the upper age limit should be for parenthood.

   b   Many people could be affected if there was a law to stop people having children.

   c   People should have the freedom to make their own decisions in life.

7 · Skills for success

PRE-READING **You are going to read a text about interview techniques. Read the questions and choose the best answers.**

1 The interviewer asks, 'What is your greatest weakness?' Should you ...

   a choose a weakness that most employees are likely to have?

   b mention a weak point that has nothing to do with that job?

   c be honest, but say what proactive steps you took to overcome it?

2 The interviewer asks, 'Why do you want to work here?' Should you ...

   a mention some of the key messages on the company's website?

   b talk about your interest in the company's culture and brand image?

   c say you know the company has good opportunities for promotion?

3 The interviewer asks, 'Where do you want to be in five years' time?' Should you express an interest in ...

   a reaching a management position within the company?

   b establishing your own company in a similar field?

   c updating your skills through training and attending seminars?

4 During the interview, should you ...

   a avoid looking directly into the interviewer's eyes?

   b have eye contact for most of the time you are conversing?

   c only look at the interviewer when he asks a direct question?

5 At what stage should you enquire about salary?

   a during the application process

   b at the end of the interview

   c when a job offer is made

6 When writing your CV, should you ...

   a include a section on your interests?

   b put your earliest qualifications before later qualifications?

   c use a specific format for graduates?

How to get your foot in the door

In your final year or just graduated? Looking for that first real job? Read our guide and find out how to impress a potential employer.

A The position you are applying for and the kind of company you are applying to will dictate which skills and attributes are most desirable. However, the following set are consistently popular with employers.
- self-motivated
- team player
- sound academic achievement
- flexible and adaptable
- analytical skills
- ethical (in a professional sense)
- strong interpersonal communication skills
- basic computer skills

Consider which of the above would be most valuable to your employer and focus on these during the application and interview stages.

B This is a key marketing tool, so it's worth spending time and effort on producing the best piece of self-promotion possible. There is no proper format, but make sure you have clear headings, that it is concise, and free from any kind of error. You should identify the needs of your prospective employer. This will help you to work out what to include, what to highlight, and what is irrelevant. Under each heading, list your qualifications (and work experience if you have any) in reverse chronological order. Do not omit a section on your interests. Employers actually find this kind of information very useful as it can provide them with an idea of an applicant's personality. They will use this to decide how you might fit into an existing team.

C Once the company has received your CV and offers you an interview, it's time you did some serious investigation. This doesn't just mean that you visit the company's website and parrot back the contents of the 'About ...' page. Instead, search the Internet for newspaper articles, go to the library for industry journals, and talk to any contacts who know the company. Find out about the company's objectives, its culture, its brand image, and its competition. If you can refer to these, you will persuade the interviewer that you are genuinely interested in working for the company.

D Whatever you've done, there's bound to be something you've learnt that can be mentioned during an interview. If you've been employed in the catering industry, or done temp or factory work, you are sure to have gained some understanding of what it means to be part of a team. Perhaps you even acquired some leadership skills during this time. If you've worked in a bar or served up hamburgers, you'll have had face-to-face experience with customers, which is the first step in developing a sense of customer relations. Did you work in a stressful environment where you had to keep calm and prioritize tasks? Did you ever consider how, if it were your business, you would run it more effectively? All this can work to your advantage in an interview.

E When you finally meet the interviewer, a smile and a handshake always go down well, and it's good etiquette to wait to be invited to take a seat. During your conversation, don't cross your arms as this is a very defensive body position. Maintain good eye contact – this shows you are confident and honest. When you are replying to a question, don't make the mistake of talking endlessly, and avoid vague statements such as 'I want a management position one day.' If you are a graduate with limited work experience, saying that you are keen to improve your skills and abilities through in-house training and external seminars will stand you in good stead.

F An area that employers love to inquire about and candidates are reluctant to discuss concerns the job-seeker's weak points. If you play safe and just mention something that many people suffer from, you will not stand out. Something that is irrelevant to the job (for example, I'm not very good at remembering birthdays) shows you are not focusing on the company's requirements. It's better to be truthful, but also give concrete examples of things you have done to improve the situation. And when the interviewer invites you to ask your own questions at the end of the interview, it's acceptable to enquire about perks and pension plans, but do not ask about salary until the position is offered. At this stage, you will be in a better position to negotiate.

COMPREHENSION 1   **Match the headings 1–8 to the correct paragraph (A–F) in the text. There are two headings you do not need to use.**

1   Face to face: how to make the right impression

2   Beware of over-preparing your answers

3   Do your research and you'll do yourself a favour

4   Essential qualities an employer is seeking

5   Practise and improve your interview technique

6   How to ensure your CV works for you

7   How to deal appropriately with tricky questions

8   Make the most of any part-time or low-paid jobs

COMPREHENSION 2 **Read the text again and find the answers to Pre-Reading on page 72.**

1 = _____   **4** = _____

Line number(s): _____   Line number(s): _____

2 = _____   **5** = _____

Line number(s): _____   Line number(s): _____

3 = _____   **6** = _____

Line number(s): _____   Line number(s): _____

COMPREHENSION 3 **Answer the questions.**

1 What is the meaning of *dictate* in line 4?

   a To tell someone exactly what to do and how to behave.

   b To influence or control how something is done.

   c To say the words of a document that someone else writes for you.

2 How can you rewrite *list your qualifications ... in reverse chronological order* (lines 23–24)?

   List your qualifications by putting the most recent one _____ and the most distant one _____.

3 In lines 30–31, what is the meaning of *parrot back the contents of the 'About ...' page*?

   a Repeat what you read or heard without understanding it properly.

   b Mention the same things that all the other candidates referred to.

   c Highlight the basic contents, but avoid going into detail.

4 In line 37, what does *bound* mean?

   a is sure to be   **b** might be   **c** won't be

5 In lines 49–50, what is the best explanation of *a smile and a handshake always go down well*?

   A smile and a handshake ...

   a must be given first.   **b** should be done properly.

   c make a good impression.

6 In line 58, how can you rewrite *will stand you in good stead*?

   Saying you are keen to improve your skills will ...

   a put you in a favourable position when the interviewer makes a decision.

   b make it seem that you are trying too hard to impress the interviewer.

   c show you are in need of training before becoming a manager.

7 In lines 60–61, what is the meaning of *play safe?*

    a pretend to be the same

    b avoid taking a risk

    c do not consider the question carefully

8 In line 62, what is the meaning of *stand out*?

    a To be easily noticed among the other candidates

    b To show that you respect the interviewer's intelligence

    c To give an answer that is relevant to the question

9 In line 65, what are *concrete examples?*

    Examples that ...

    a can be checked by the interviewer.

    b show you are a reliable person.

    c are based on facts and information.

10 In line 69, how can you rewrite *At this stage, you will be in a better position to negotiate?*

    You can negotiate your salary ...

    a during the interview.

    b at the end of the interview.

    c when you are offered a job.

VOCABULARY SKILLS 1

flexible

reluctant

Match the adjectives (1–6) to a definition (a–f).

1 motivated

2 flexible

3 valuable

4 analytical

5 ethical

6 reluctant

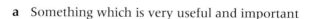

a Something which is very useful and important

b Using a method of separating things into their parts in order to examine and understand them

c Not willing to do something

d Enthusiastic and determined to achieve success

e Willing to make changes or to accept a situation that is changing

f Behaving in a way that is morally correct

VOCABULARY SKILLS 2

Change the form of the word in **bold** to complete the sentences.

1 To be a good leader, you also need to be a _____. **motivated**

2 We didn't hire James Taylor as he seemed rather _____. **flexible**

3 Felicia's background and experience will be absolutely _____ when we set up our new factory in Poland. **valuable**

4 Claudie is applying for a job as an economic _____. **analytical**

5 In my opinion, it's _____ to lie on a CV. **ethical**

6 Sarah expressed her _____ to relocate to Paris. **reluctant**

Grammar	*Once the company offers you an interview, **it's time you did** some serious investigation.*
Time versus tense	We use *It's time* + past simple to say that something is very important or urgent, and must be done immediately.
	*If you've worked in a bar … you **will have had** face-to-face experience with customers.*
	We can use the future perfect simple to express certainty about a past situation or event.

GRAMMAR 1

What would you say in these situations?

For example:

The office secretary left the job a week ago. *It's time we …*

It's time we employed someone else.

1 You think the software in the office is old. *It's time we …*

2 A friend of yours really hates his job. *It's time you …*

3 You are still at the office and it's very late. *It's time I …*

4 You are still waiting for a report from one of your team. *It's time you …*

5 You are still working at the age of 70. *It's time I …*

6 The printer broke down again this morning. *It's time we …*

GRAMMAR 2

Which sentences express certainty about the past?

1 Our clients will have received the new brochure by now.

2 By the end of this course, you will have learnt everything there is to know about marketing.

3 I will have attended five interviews by the time I graduate.

4 Sue is so clever she will have got an A grade in all her exams.

5 I'm sure she will have decided which candidate to employ.

6 I reckon I will have read a hundred applications by lunchtime.

Effective • *Skills*

You are going to read an interview with an Egyptian student who is talking about his work. Translate the words in **bold**. Then tick (✔) three statements that you think the student makes.

1 ☐ At business school, I got a diploma in **event management**. _____

2 ☐ I don't think **marketing** is very important in business. _____

3 ☐ Our schools are divided by **gender**. _____

4 ☐ Business and politics are **inseparable**. _____

5 ☐ One wedding we organized had a **nautical theme**. _____

6 ☐ There is a wonderful **aquarium** in Alexandria. _____

7 ☐ We printed the **company logo** at the top of the page. _____

8 ☐ We tried hard not to be too **unconventional**. _____

Complete the sentences with the words in the box. Use a dictionary to help you.

| absolutely vital | close-knit | our biggest market |
| their big day | spectacular | agenda |

1 It is important that your _____ covers everything you want to discuss.

2 I come from a very _____ family. We still see each other all the time.

3 The bride and groom are often extremely nervous on _____.

4 The opening ceremony for the Olympic games was _____.

5 If you want to succeed in business, it is _____ to plan ahead.

6 The United States is _____. We sell more to them than to anyone else.

Find the same words in the interview to review your answers.

Student profile Ahmad Badawi

I: (A) _____
A: Yeah, actually I was thinking of doing business. I didn't really have much of an idea of what, but I knew I wanted to start some kind of company, so I went to business school and ended up getting a diploma in
5 event management.

I: (B) _____
A: Oh, they taught us everything there is to know about business, including how to set one up, how to advertise, how to do the marketing. It was very thorough and I learnt such a lot about the work you have to do behind the
10 scenes. Things like the research you need to do beforehand and the long-term planning that is **absolutely vital**.

I: (C) _____
A: Well in our community, functions are often divided by gender. If there are women involved, like at a wedding, you have to have a lady to organize
15 that side of things. So I was looking for a female business partner. I was very lucky because I had a close woman friend who I grew up with. Our families have always been very **close knit** and we have been inseparable for as long as I can remember. So she was the perfect person to join me. She is in charge of everything now, while I'm here in New Zealand.

20 **I**: (D) _____
A: Not really. In Egypt, people like to have someone to organize their events for them, so that is very good for us. They just say, 'I'm getting married, you organize it.'

I: (E) _____
25 **A**: Yes, that's probably **our biggest market**. People come to us and ask for ideas. I usually start by asking them what they have always dreamt about for **their big day**. Sometimes their ideas are a little bit boring and we try to encourage them to take some risks because for me the best thing about the job is to strive for something new and unusual, something that no one
30 has ever done before.

I: (F) _____
A: We had a couple once, who knew exactly what they wanted. The woman loved the sea. She lived in Alexandria on the coast and wanted her wedding to have a nautical theme. Now, in Egypt most women wear white
35 at their weddings, very similar to a western wedding. But she wanted blue. So we made her a beautiful sky-blue dress and painted the walls of the hall

dark blue and put lots of sand on the floor. All the tablecloths were blue and the plates were white like sea-shells. Then, all around the walls we built an enormous aquarium and filled it with fish so the room felt like we
40 were all under water. It was **spectacular** but very expensive!

I: (G) _____
A: We do birthdays, and we do meetings sometimes. Actually, when we started we did a lot of meetings. There are lots of small companies in my country that have very small offices and they don't have much space for
45 meetings. So usually they go to a coffee shop and obviously that's not a very good look. So we would rent a bigger room for them and manage everything.

I: (H) _____
A: We organized all the refreshments they needed and any stationery, and sometimes we would even help them write the **agenda** and have it
50 printed with their company logo at the top.

I: (I) _____
A: Yes, because everyone who came to us wanted to see what we had done before and of course we had nothing to show them. So we started by arranging business meetings for free, and then after a while our reputation
55 grew, and then we started charging.

I: (J) _____
A: Well, I want to study marketing and public relations here, and when I go back to Egypt I want to open another business alongside my business, maybe in marketing or advertising.

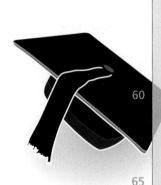

60 **I**: (K) _____
A: I think I have great imagination and I always try to approach my work from different angles. To me, it's a waste of time to repeat what someone else has already done. I try and look for the unconventional approach. If I'm selling a soft drink I don't want to show people drinking it. For me,
65 it's better if they throw it at each other. I like to do something a little bit strange to make it more interesting.

SCANNING 1 **Read the interview again and review your answers to Activating vocabulary 1 on page 78.**

SCANNING 2 **Match the interviewer's questions to Ahmad's answers.**

1 What other events do you manage?

2 So what are your plans for the future?

3 Do you have any problems finding customers?

4   So, do you do a lot of weddings?

5   Ahmad, what did you do when you left school?

6   What sort of services did you provide?

7   And what did you learn on your course?

8   How did you go about setting up your business?

9   What do you see as your greatest strength?

10   Was it difficult to find customers at first?

11   What was the craziest idea you ever heard?

ANALYZING MEANING

Decide if the information about the text is True (T), False (F), or Not Given (NG). Write T, F, or NG.

1   Ahmad specialized in advertising and marketing. ☐

2   People in Egypt don't have time to organize their own weddings. ☐

3   The woman from Alexandria wore a typical Egyptian wedding dress. ☐

4   Egyptian business people like to have good coffee at meetings. ☐

5   Experience is valued by Ahmad's clients. ☐

6   Ahmad's company makes a bigger profit by trying different and unusual things. ☐

VOCABULARY EXTENSION

In lines 45-46, the phrase *that's not a good look* could be replaced with …

a   that's not a comfortable place.

b   that doesn't create a good impression.

c   that isn't a typical place for meetings.

DISCUSSION

Discuss this question with a partner.

Ahmad talks about taking an **unconventional approach** to his work. What are the advantages and disadvantages of taking an unconventional approach to life? Think about these areas:

- family   • study   • friends   • boyfriend/girlfriend   • work

- food   • meeting people   • travel   • anything else

8 • The paranormal

PRE-READING 1   **What do you know about these things from the text? Choose the best answers. Discuss your answers with a partner.**

1 The Yeti is supposed to be a *huge / tiny / human-like / lizard-like* creature from *the Himalayas / the Alps*.

2 The Loch Ness Monster is supposed to be a *long-legged / long-necked* monster living in a *forest / lake* in *Ireland / Scotland*.

3 Crop circles were once thought to be *patterns / messages* in *rocks / corn fields* by *aliens / ancient civilizations*.

4 Weeping statues are supposed to produce *water / blood* from their *eyes / hands*.

PRE-READING 2   **Match the words in bold in the text to a definition.**

1 _____ = the practice of putting someone into a state similar to sleep in which they can still hear and react to suggestions

2 _____ = events or situations that can be seen to happen or exist

3 _____ = a trick in which someone deliberately tells people that something is true when it is not

4 _____ = the feeling you have when you are frightened

5 _____ = a signal or stimulus that people respond to

6 _____ = the act of taking someone away from their home, family, etc. using force

7 _____ = someone who has doubts about things that other people think are true or right

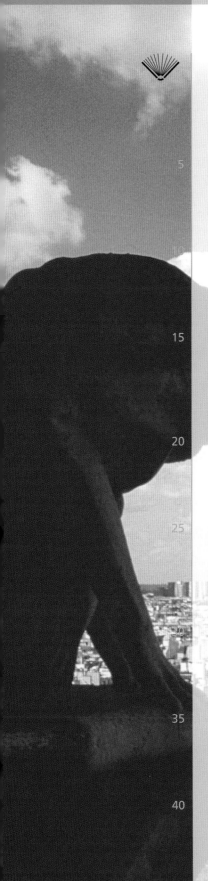

Fear and fakes

In 2004, a film called *The Village* was released. We see a small rural community in 1897 whose inhabitants live by candlelight once the sun sets and have no means of communicating with the outside world. At night, they can see the terrifying shapes of strange creatures in the forest and hear their blood-curdling screams. No one has ever come face to face with these monsters; in fact it is their **fear** that keeps them prisoner. Little do they realize that the rest of the world is living in the 21st century and the monsters are not what they seem. But the point is that not until the advent of electric lights, telephones, and decent infrastructure did people become less superstitious and overcome their suspicion of the world beyond the boundaries of their village. Fear of the unknown has always had a deep psychological effect on the human imagination. It is not surprising then that our history is so full of tales of the supernatural and sightings of the paranormal.

Most cultures once had a belief in some form of ghost, magic, or monsters, and unexplained **phenomena** continued to hold some fascination until quite recently. In the 1970s, the Yeti and the Loch Ness Monster competed for media coverage, and the owners of haunted ancestral homes opened their doors to the curious, paying public. Indeed, the more ghosts you claimed to have, the more visitors were likely to pay. Aliens and UFOs have popped up on a regular basis since the early 1940s, and more recently we have seen on the evening news pictures of crying Madonna statues and complex crop circles in remote wheat fields. The latest craze is for TV psychics, a bunch of charismatic characters who stun members of the audience with revelations that can only come from dead relatives. Or so they would have you believe. **Sceptics** would first look for a rational explanation – and can usually find one.

Let us turn first to ghosts. Sceptics have proposed a number of theories to explain the spooky encounters some people have. According to Dr Richard Wiseman, of the University of Hertfordshire, England, people often respond to environmental **cues** without realizing it. Dr Wiseman, who carried out his research at supposedly haunted buildings in Britain, found, for instance, that if there is a slight draft in the room, or a change in light intensity or temperature, people may imagine they have 'felt a presence' – especially if they had prior knowledge that the place was known to be haunted. Dr Paul Stevens from Edinburgh University has carried out experiments to show that the Earth's magnetic field can influence human physiology, which may explain why so-called hauntings occur repeatedly in the same

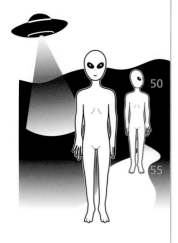

place. Other scientists believe that certain sound waves, which are beyond our hearing ability, can cause hallucinations and small vibrations – leading people to believe they have experienced a visit from the dead.

As for UFO sightings, about 80 per cent of these are believed to be cases of mistaken identity. In fact, people are looking at either Jupiter or Venus, or some other astral body that they have never noticed before. Aeroplanes, flocks of birds, or even clouds have also often confused observers. Alien **abductions**, in which the victim is taken away on a spaceship, seem to be especially prevalent in the United States. This may partly be explained by the doubtful use of **hypnosis** to help people 'recover lost memories.' This technique has been proven to give people false or distorted memories, as the hypnotist is, in fact, planting ideas in the subject's mind, rather than enabling them to recall forgotten events. There also seems to be an upsurge in abductions and sightings whenever a new 'alien series' is shown on TV. Interestingly enough, now that the world seems more preoccupied with war, terrorism, and superbugs, there has been a sharp decline in reported abductions and sightings. It seems that one fear has been replaced by others.

Sceptical scientists are particularly scathing of TV psychics and mediums. The difference between them is that the psychics claim to be talking to our deceased friends and relatives, whereas mediums also have their own spirit guide – usually someone who lived many centuries ago. Oddly enough, that spirit is fluent in the language of the medium and seems to have forgotten his or her own. There is a very simple explanation for the apparent gift of these two groups. Both rely on a technique called 'cold reading' which relies on the laws of probability. For example, any middle-aged person will have at least one dead relative, probably more. There are a limited number of names that are popular with each generation. So, when the psychic asks 'Does anyone know a William in that part of the audience?' the chances are extremely high that someone will. They also depend on subjects that have relevance to most people: babies, weddings, back pain, a sudden death, illness, hospital. And it is easy to manipulate people with questions such as 'Did your mother die young?' If the answer is 'No,' their reply is 'I thought not,' and if 'Yes,' then 'I thought so.' Borrow a book on cold reading and try it for yourself.

85 | There is one more explanation for mysterious lights in the sky, odd-shaped footprints, crop circles, and so on: the **hoax**. Hoaxers do it for the sense of power, for the publicity (when they finally confess), and even for revenge. But all of them must find a gawping, gasping public rather amusing. If you share their sense of humour, I recommend you visit the inspirational www.museumofhoaxes.com. Not only will you discover the truth behind some fabulous practical jokes, but it might give you a few ideas of your own!

COMPREHENSION 1   **Answer the questions. Use your own words as far as possible.**

1   According to the writer, what is it that really keeps people trapped in the village?

_____

2   What reasons does the writer give to explain people's change in attitude to an unfamiliar world?

_____

3   What does the writer imply about the owners of haunted buildings?

_____

4   According to Dr Wiseman, what environmental cues make people believe they have had a ghostly experience?

_____

5   What other two reasons are given in paragraph 3 to explain hauntings?

_____

6   What three reasons are given to explain people's belief that they have seen a UFO or been abducted by an alien?

_____

7   According to the writer, why are far fewer sightings and abductions being reported?

_____

8   What does the writer find particularly strange about the spirits that mediums claim to be talking to?

_____

9   How does the technique of cold reading work?

_____

10   Why does the writer suggest you visit the website? (two reasons)

_____

COMPREHENSION 2   **Answer the questions.**

1   In line 7, what is the meaning of *Little do they realize*?

The villagers ...

a   have suspected this for a while.

b   have no idea.

c   have just begun to realize this.

2   In lines 17–18, what does *hold some fascination* mean?

Some unexplained phenomena continued ...

a   to create interest.

b   to deceive people.

c   to receive media attention.

3   ... *the Yeti and the Loch Ness Monster competed for media coverage.* (lines 18–19)

a   What is *media coverage*?

b   In what sense would these creatures compete?

4   In line 22, what meaning does *popped up* give to the sentence?

a   Many films have been made about aliens and UFOs since the 1940s.

b   Interest in aliens and UFOs has declined and then increased since the 1940s.

c   People have been surprised by the number of newspaper stories about aliens and UFOs since the 1940s.

5   In line 26, what is the meaning of *stun*?

a   shock   b   entertain   c   lie to

6   In line 28, what is the function of the phrase *Or so they would have you believe*?

a   It rejects the previous claim.

b   It suggests a likely result.

c   It emphasizes purpose.

7   In line 47, what does *these* refer to?

8   In lines 80-81, what does the writer mean by *Borrow a book on cold reading and try it for yourself*?

a   Find out if you have any level of psychic ability.

b   Learn how to make people believe you have psychic powers.

c   Discover ways to recognize real psychics from fake ones.

VOCABULARY SKILLS 1

Find words with these meanings in the text.

1 The introduction of a new product, idea, custom. (*n*) (lines 5–10)

2 Having a strong personal quality that makes people like you. (*adj*) (lines 25–29)

3 Frightening in a way that makes you nervous because it involves things that do not seem natural and cannot be explained by science. (*adj*) (lines 30–35)

4 Something that you think you can see or hear that is not really there. (*n*) (lines 40–45)

5 Changed so that something is no longer true or accurate. (*adj*) (lines 50–55)

6 A sudden increase in something. (*n*) (lines 55–60)

7 A formal word for *dead*. (*adj*) (lines 60–65)

8 To influence or control someone in a clever or dishonest way. (*v*) (lines 75–80)

Something that you think you can see or hear that is not really there.

VOCABULARY SKILLS 2

Complete the sentences with the answers to Vocabulary skills 1.

For example:

You need to be quite _charismatic_ if you want to be a chat show host.

1 When people are in the desert, they often experience _____ due to dehydration.

2 Simon is very clever at _____ his parents – he always gets his way.

3 The _____ of the MP3 player has changed the way people listen to music.

4 Jane's _____ grandmother left her a beautiful necklace in her will.

5 The _____ in unemployment was caused by a high number of imports.

6 Some journalists _____ the truth to make their stories more interesting.

7 I never walk home past the cemetery – it's too _____.

Grammar	***Little do they realize*** *that the rest of the world is living in the 21st century.* ***Not until*** *the advent of electric lights, telephones and decent infrastructure **did people become** less superstitious.*
Inversion after negative adverbials	*Little* and *not until* can come first in a clause to give more emphasis or make the style of writing more dramatic. The subject and verb are then inverted. If there is no auxiliary verb, *do/does/did* are used. Other common negative adverbials are: *Hardly ... when/Never (before)/No sooner ... than/Rarely*

GRAMMAR 1   <u>Underline</u> the correct structure.

1   *Little did the audience members suspect / Little suspected the audience members / Little the audience members did suspect* they were being tricked.

2   *No sooner have the lights gone out / No sooner the lights had gone out / No sooner had the lights gone out* than we heard a spooky noise.

3   Hardly *had / was / have* the first episode of the series *appearing / appear / appeared* on TV when the number of reported abductions suddenly rose.

GRAMMAR 2   Tick (✔) the sentences that are correct. Correct the sentences that are wrong.

1   The radio broadcast warned people that aliens were coming and created panic. Never before have so many people fallen for one hoax.

2   Hardly had entered the old house than we heard the awful scream.

3   No sooner the strange lights had appear in the sky than they disappeared again.

4   Not until was recently it revealed how crop circles were really made.

5   Little did we know that the ghost was actually the castle owner in disguise.

6   I went to see a psychic show last week. Rarely have I seen such obvious manipulation of people's emotions.

SPEAKING   Discuss the questions with a partner.

1   Do you agree with the sceptics or do you think ghosts really exist?

2   Do you believe that aliens have visited the Earth? Why?/Why not?

3   What is your opinion of people who claim to predict the future?

4   What other supernatural or paranormal phenomena do you know about?

Effective • *Skills*

DRACULA

This story is set in 1875. A young lawyer called Jonathan Harker and an old professor, Van Helsing, must find a way to destroy the vampire, Dracula.

Arthur, Jonathan and Van Helsing went to the churchyard late that night. Lucy West had been buried in the family vault in the churchyard.
5 The Professor was carrying a large bag. Arthur opened the vault with his key. The three men stood quietly around Lucy's coffin. 'Look carefully,' the Professor said. 'The vault has not been opened since Lucy's funeral, has it? Now, watch!' Then, with a long piece of iron, Van Helsing began to open Lucy's coffin. 'There,' he said as he lifted the lid.

10 At first, Arthur did not want to look. Lucy had been dead for nearly two weeks. Then he gave a terrible cry. 'My God! The coffin is empty!' he shouted. 'Where is my wife?'

'I can answer that,' Jonathan said quietly. 'Lucy needs blood. She is looking for another victim!'

15 'It is true,' Van Helsing said. 'Let us wait in the churchyard for Lucy to come back.' They left the vault and Arthur locked it again. Van Helsing led them to a dark part of the churchyard. They waited. The time passed very slowly. Then, in the moonlight, they saw something white move towards Lucy's vault. Arthur gave a cry and stepped forward. 'My God, it
20 is Lucy!' he shouted.

The thing turned its head and looked straight at them. The moon was very bright and the three friends could see everything clearly. What they saw filled them with fear. Yes, it was Lucy. Her face and long, dark hair looked the same. But the eyes shone with a terrible red light. Blood was
25 running from her red lips onto her white dress. She smiled and they could see her sharp, white teeth.

'Arthur, my love, come to me,' she whispered. She held out her hands and walked towards him. 'Come to me now, and never, never leave me.'

30　Arthur took another step forward. Lucy opened out her arms to hold him. Van Helsing ran in front of Arthur and held up a large cross. When Lucy saw the cross, she stopped smiling. Her face became cruel and angry. She made a noise like an animal and ran towards the vault. It was shut and locked, but the vampire disappeared inside.

'Oh, God! Was that terrible thing my Lucy?' Arthur cried.

35　'That is not the dear woman you loved,' Van Helsing told him. 'It is the vampire that is using her body. But if we are strong, we can help Lucy rest peacefully. Give me my bag, Jonathan.' They entered the vault again. It was almost dawn. When Van Helsing opened the coffin, they saw the vampire. Her eyes were open and she smiled at them. It was a
40　terrible smile.

Van Helsing opened his bag. He took out a long, sharp stake and a hammer. Then he looked at Arthur. 'I shall hold the stake and point it at her heart,' the Professor said. 'Then, as we pray, hammer it down.'

With a last look at the coffin, Arthur raised the hammer. He brought
45　it down – once, twice, many times. Terrible screams came from the vampire's blood-covered lips. The white dress became as red as the stake that went into Lucy's body. They all prayed. At last, the thing in the coffin stopped moving. Arthur dropped the hammer and almost fainted. 'Look,' Van Helsing said. 'Now she is at peace.'

50　There, in the coffin, lay Lucy. She was dead and at peace. All the blood had gone and there was a beautiful smile on her face. 'Now you can kiss your wife,' Van Helsing said. Arthur kissed Lucy once on the lips. Then he turned and left the vault. Van Helsing and Jonathan worked together. They cut off Lucy's head. Then they closed the coffin lid and hammered
55　it down. When they left the vault, it was daylight. Birds were singing and the air was warm.

'We have begun our work,' Van Helsing said to Jonathan and Arthur, 'but we have not finished it. Now we must find Count Dracula. We must destroy him forever.'

ANALYZING
MEANING

Decide if the information about the text is True (T), False (F), or Not Given (NG). Write T, F, or NG.

1 Arthur did not know where they were going in the churchyard. ☐

2 Arthur did not want to look at the body of Lucy at first. ☐

3 Jonathan believed that Lucy had gone to find Dracula. ☐

4 A white creature was carrying Lucy's body back to the vault. ☐

5 Lucy appeared to look exactly the same as when she was alive. ☐

6 When Lucy called Arthur, he knew she still loved him. ☐

7 Van Helsing's cross caused the vampire in Lucy to feel pain. ☐

8 Arthur refused to help Van Helsing destroy the vampire in Lucy. ☐

9 Lucy's body started to disappear once the vampire had been destroyed. ☐

10 Jonathan and Arthur believed the battle with Dracula was over. ☐

RECOGNIZING
KEY WORDS AND
MAIN IDEAS

Complete the summary with Jonathan Harker's words. Write no more than two words for each gap.

'It was late when we got to the (**1**)_____. Arthur had the key to the (**2**)_____ and let us in. At first, we just stood there, silently, next to the (**3**)_____, but then the Professor opened it up and Lucy wasn't there. She was probably somewhere hunting for a new (**4**)_____. Anyway, we went outside to wait for her. There was enough (**5**)_____ for us to see her come back. You can't imagine how terrible her eyes were – they were filled with this strange (**6**)_____. Arthur couldn't keep quiet and she saw us. She tried to make Arthur go to her, but Van Helsing made her run away with a (**7**)_____. She disappeared and got back into her coffin. Van Helsing told us to (**8**)_____ while we destroyed the vampire. Arthur used a (**9**)_____ to bang a stake in her heart until the vampire was gone. Arthur gave Lucy a final (**10**)_____ and then he left. I'm afraid, though, that the battle isn't over yet.'

EXERCISE 1

Read two advertisements from a university noticeboard.

Head off for your first work experience!

Looking for a useful and enjoyable way to try out your new degree or just putting off a nine-to-five job? Why not take a year out to think about it and sign up with VSO (Voluntary Service Overseas), an organization that sends volunteers to help out with community projects in Africa (Poverty Alleviation, Sustainable Livelihoods), Asia (Environment, Health and Education), and The Pacific (Rural Development and Empowering Women). If you are seeking adventure and want to do some good at the same time, working alongside an excellent team of like-minded people could be just the experience you are looking for. Both the work and the **camaraderie** can be extremely **rewarding**. Accommodation / flights / and visas are provided. Volunteers should be **adaptable**, open to new cultures and be prepared to work in basic conditions. For more information, come and see Steve Dunn in the Student Union from 9am–12pm Mon–Thurs.

ATTENTION LAW STUDENTS

The Innocence Project was first established in the United States. It aims to re-examine criminal cases in which a wrongful conviction may have occurred. Participating students are expected to thoroughly analyze witness statements and take a fresh look at evidence, searching for details that the original attorney may have missed. It can be **painstaking** work, but the Innocence Project has helped people gain both their freedom and **compensation** for wrongful imprisonment. Furthermore, through studying these cases, you will learn to identify injustices in current legal procedure and see how to correct them. This is unpaid work that requires a **commitment** of about 16 hours a week, but it is a chance to gain your first real practical experience in the field of law. Talk to Jane Andrews in the Student Law Office if you are interested.

EXERCISE 2

Which of the following statements applies to which advertisement? Write **A** for the first advertisement, **B** for the second advertisement, or **A/B** for both advertisements.

1 You will be able to recognize how the system could be improved. ☐

2 You don't mind working without modern facilities. ☐

3 You will work with other people who are similar to you.

4 You will have to work slowly and carefully. ☐

5 You will have the opportunity to do something useful, while deciding what kind of job you want. ☐

6 You will not earn a salary for the work you do. ☐

EXERCISE 3

Which of the words in **bold** in the text means ...

1 friendship and trust between a group of people?

2 something that is done very slowly and carefully?

3 a duty or responsibility that you have accepted?

4 giving you satisfaction and pleasure?

5 money that someone receives because something bad happened to them?

6 able to change ideas or behaviour easily in order to deal with new situations?

EXERCISE 1

Read the questions in Exercise 2 first. Then read the text as quickly as possible to find the answers.

The haunted house

For me, most paranormal phenomena can be, or will someday be, explained by science, and I'm extremely **sceptical** when it comes to ghosts. When people report a haunting, I think they probably experienced a form of **hallucination** or a **hoax**. Having said that, when I was about 13 years old, my brother, my mother, and I went to stay with my aunt Christine. Her family lives in a huge country mansion that they bought very cheaply after it had been **abandoned** for many years. At the time, they lived in one wing of the house and guests stayed in the opposite wing. In between the wings was the middle part of the house, which was just room after dusty room, filled with odd things that my uncle had brought home, like old pianos, broken statues, and rusty clocks. You could explore for the whole day and not bump into anyone else, apart from the occasional peacock that had jumped in through an open window, or a rat that my cousins had tamed. Anyway, the room where I was staying was at the end of a long corridor, and I have to admit that I did feel the atmosphere was a bit **spooky**. The floors creaked and there was a rocking chair in the room which you always see in horror films! But one night, I suddenly woke up and opened my eyes, thinking my brother had come into the room and was sitting on my legs. I could feel an incredible weight on both of them, but the room was filled with moonlight and I could see nobody was there. I was **petrified** and just closed my eyes tight and waited for what seemed like an eternity before I felt the weight lift. In the morning, I told my brother, who thought it was absolutely hilarious. My aunt's brother, however, who happened to be visiting, thought differently. He had had exactly the same experience in the same room, and was also **at a loss** to explain what had really happened. I know it's not **rational**, but nothing could persuade me to sleep there again!

EXERCISE 2

Decide if the sentences are True (T), False (F), or if the information is Not Given (NG) in the text.

1 Christine's ancestors had owned the house for many years before she lived there. ☐

2 The author's uncle collected strange things in order to sell them. ☐

3 It was possible to spend a day in the house without seeing another person. ☐

4 The author's brother tried to frighten her by sitting on her legs. ☐

5 The author stayed still for a long time before the pressure on her legs went away. ☐

6 Christine's brother convinced the author that her experience had been a hoax. ☐

EXERCISE 3

Translate the words and phrases in **bold** in the text.

9. Body and spirit

PRE-READING 1 Match the words in the box to the situations below. Use a dictionary to help you. You can use the same words more than once.

> severe injuries   shock   disorientated
> blood loss   frostbite   dehydration   exhausted
> starvation   hypothermia   hallucinating

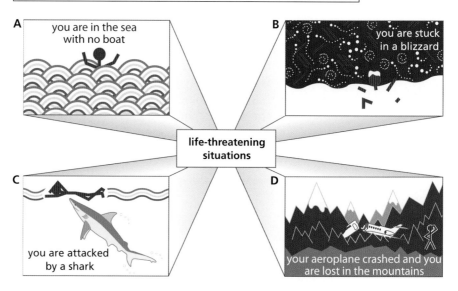

A you are in the sea with no boat

B you are stuck in a blizzard

life-threatening situations

C you are attacked by a shark

D your aeroplane crashed and you are lost in the mountains

PRE-READING 2 Read the first paragraph of the text. What is the author's aim?

1 To prove that dangerous situations occur more frequently than most of us realize.

2 To compare the quality of advice that survival programmes offer.

3 To suggest that people question their own survival skills.

What if ...?

Flick through the TV channels and there are any number of TV programmes dealing with the theme of survival. There are the lightweight reality shows with a group of contestants you wouldn't want to spend five minutes with at the bus stop, let alone a whole

5 month on an island. There are also the more factual shows in which an expert shows you how to make a tent from banana leaves and shoelaces, and the best way to fry beetles – just in case you are ever shipwrecked or lost in the jungle.

What does the popularity of this kind of programme tell us? Despite
10 the **convenient** gadgets, tools, and technology of the modern age, we are aware that possibly, just possibly, we could end up in a situation without them. We also know that man is not always in control of nature (think tsunamis, earthquakes, volcanic eruptions, landslides) or human nature (think plane crashes due to pilot error,
15 a bus driver falling asleep at the wheel). We often ask: what would I do if that happened to me? Would I survive? If you have attended a survival skills course, that might help, but what if you haven't?

It was his background in the Navy as a diver that helped save New Zealander Robert Hewitt's life after he spent 75 hours in the freezing
20 open sea. In February 2006, he was diving for seafood near Mana Island off the Wellington coast, when he was suddenly swept away from his boat. He knew it was foolish to swim against the tide, so he let himself float. Soon he began to suffer the effects of hypothermia and dehydration. Nevertheless, he was **determined** to survive. He
25 got some protein from the raw seafood in his catch bag and sucked at the mist in his oxygen tank. He also thought of his fiancée and children, and would call out, 'I love you' to keep himself going. When he was finally rescued, he thought he was hallucinating.

Not everyone, however, caught in a life or death situation, has the
30 advantage of training. In August 1990, Joji (George) Iwama made a solo climb of Mount Ruapehu and after reaching the summit, dug out a snow cave to spend the night in. He was getting ready to descend the next morning when, to his horror, a snowstorm hit. Determined to get down, George went out into the blizzard,
35 believing he could manage with a compass and map. It wasn't long before he became disoriented, frostbitten, and exhausted. He made a second snow cave and sealed himself in. Listening to his radio, he heard about the deaths of some soldiers he had passed on the way up, and he also heard the announcer report that he was probably
40 dead, too, but he didn't let this dampen his spirits. He spent the next few days carefully **rationing** his food and constantly moving his

frostbitten toes. When the blizzard finally cleared, he got down the mountain. He had survived, even though those with army training hadn't. Despite the bad decision to leave the first snow cave, he was

45 able to remain calm enough to decide to build a second. It was this decision, and that **shelter**, that saved his life.

The ability to remain focused probably also saved the life of Bethany Hamilton, a 13-year-old professional surfer who was attacked by a shark off Makua Beach in Hawaii. She was lying on her board when

50 the shark suddenly bit through her left arm just below the shoulder. Despite the shock, the pain, and the blood loss, she held on to her board and the shark disappeared. She swam to shore and shouted for help. She was also saved by the quick-thinking actions of her friend's father, Holt Blanchard, who used a surf leash as a tourniquet

55 to stop the flow of blood. The attack occurred in the autumn of 2003. Today Bethany is still surfing, despite the loss of her left arm, and has become an inspiration to many young surfers.

And undoubtedly one of the most famous survival stories of all time is that of the young Uruguayan football team whose aeroplane

60 crashed in the Andes mountains in 1972. Of the 45 people on board, 16 survived for 72 days. Some people had died in the crash, while others had suffered head wounds or broken bones. These survivors had to endure freezing temperatures, and with no shoes or blankets, soon began to suffer frostbite. They were even buried inside the

65 aeroplane fuselage by a series of avalanches. Their food ran out in days. There was only one way to survive – by eating the bodies of the other passengers, and eventually,

70 all the survivors agreed to this. Horrific as this must have been, it was the only practical solution to avoid starvation. Most people

75 would say they would never do this, but most of us have never been tested in this way. Until you are, you can't be certain.

COMPREHENSION 1   Complete the table about the survivors.

Who?	Where?	When?	How did they survive?	How were they affected physically?
Robert Hewitt			1 ate raw seafood 2 3	1 2
		August 1990	1 2 3	1 2
	Makua Beach, Hawaii, USA		1 2	1 2 3
Uruguayan football team			1	1 2 3

COMPREHENSION 2   Answer the questions.

1   In line 1, what does *there are any number* tell us about the author's opinion?

    a   there are a few   **b**   there are many

2   In line 4, what is the function of *let alone*?

    It would be bad to spend five minutes with these people, but a whole month would be ...

    a   awful.   **b**   lonely.   **c**   great fun.

3   In line 27, what does this use of *would* mean?

    a   He used to say, 'I love you' all the time.

    b   He said, 'I love you' many times when he was in the water.

    c   He wanted to see his family again and say, 'I love you.'

4 In line 40, how can you rewrite the phrase *dampen his spirits*?

    a make him frightened of death

    b cause him to start seeing imaginary things

    c affect his positive mood in a harmful way

5 In line 57, what does *an inspiration to* mean?

Many young surfers admire Bethany Hamilton and have …

    a avoided

    b stopped

    c started

surfing because of her.

6 In line 71, what does *this* refer to?

7 In line 78, what words are omitted after the first clause?

Until you are …

    a being honest,

    b in a survival situation,

    c being practical, not emotional,

you can't be certain.

VOCABULARY SKILLS

Complete the sentences with the correct words.

1 *convenient / comfortable*

    a We can hold the interview whenever it's _____ for you.

    b I don't feel _____ talking about my survival story.

2 *determined / hopeful*

    a We don't know whether Mark is still alive, but we're _____.

    b We're _____ to find Mark, no matter what it takes.

3 *ration / share*

    a If we _____ our survival tips, we can help each other.

    b I _____ myself to one cup of water a day.

4 *shelter / protection*

    a On the island, we built a small _____ out of palm leaves.

    b You need a very strong cream that will offer _____ from the desert sun.

Grammar	*An expert shows you how to make a tent ... **in case** you get shipwrecked.*
In case/If	We use *in case* to show how we can prepare for a possible situation or event.
	*Quickly make a snow cave **if** a blizzard is coming.*
	We use *if* to show how we can react to a possible situation or event.

GRAMMAR **Complete the sentences with *in case* or *if*.**

1 You may have less than 30 minutes to find an antidote _____ you get bitten by a cobra.

2 You should take some antidote on holiday _____ you get bitten by a cobra.

3 You should take out some insurance _____ you have a skiing accident.

4 Use your mobile phone to call for help _____ you have a skiing accident.

5 I suggest you tell people where you're going, _____ you get lost at sea.

6 Don't try to swim ashore _____ your boat sinks.

SPEAKING **Discuss the questions with a partner.**

1 You're in a forest when you suddenly see a large bear. Do you run uphill or downhill?

2 You're in the desert and have no water. You have a plastic sheet and a drinking cup. There's no cactus around, just some small rocks. How do you find water?

3 What is the best way to put out a small forest fire?

4 What should you do if a shark attacks you?

'What should you do if a shark attacks you?'

Effective • *Skills*

INFERRING MEANING

What do you think *exorcism* means?

1 To officially say that someone can no longer be a member of the Church because they have done something to break the rules

2 The process or action of getting rid of an evil spirit, for example a ceremony or prayer

3 The act of killing a person as a punishment for a crime

The other two definitions are for *execute* and *excommunicate*. Which is which?

SCANNING 1

Scan the text for the words (a–c). Write a translation for each word. Then choose the correct word to complete the sentences.

1 **a** rabbi   **b** priest   **c** nun

In my village, our local _____ knew all the children by name, and if we didn't go to church on Sunday, he'd tell us off when he saw us in the street.

2 **a** crucifixion   **b** suffocation   **c** strangulation

The Romans killed many of their enemies using _____.
People were nailed to a wooden cross and experienced terrible pain.

3 **a** crosses   **b** relics   **c** convents

Both Buddhism and Roman Catholicism have a tradition of revering _____. The Buddha's bones and teeth were divided after his death and in the Middle Ages, many churches claimed to have the bones or personal possessions of saints.

4 **a** demon   **b** shaman   **c** disciple

A person who follows a religious leader such as the Buddha or Jesus and helps spread their message to other people is known as a _____.

SAVING S⊕ULS
at what cost?

A

Say the word *exorcism* and most people think of the 1973 Hollywood film *The Exorcist*, in which a Catholic priest attempts to drive out the demons from a young girl. Even if people don't remember the plot, they've never forgotten Regan's violent fits, the obscenities she shouted, and the way her head spun 360 degrees!

B

Now jump forward to Romania, 2005, where a **nun** is gagged and tied to a **cross**, then left for three days in a cold room in the **convent** where she lives. She is said to have died through **suffocation** as a cloth had been stuffed in her mouth, but the **priest** who ordered the **crucifixion** as part of an exorcism claims she was saved from the devil. Unlike the film, this was an actual event and the priest was accused of murder by the police.

C

The notion of driving out spirits from a person, place, or object may have originated in ancient **shamanistic** beliefs and we can see types of exorcism in several faiths. In Judaism, there are references to the *dybbuk* – the good or bad spirits of dead people who enter the bodies of the living in order to pursue their business on Earth. However, **rabbis** see exorcism as a form of healing for both possessor and possessed. In Islam, a person can free themselves of evil spirits, called *jinn*, by reciting parts of the Koran.

D

It is the Roman Catholic Church, however, which is most known for the practice of exorcism. There are biblical references to Jesus driving out **demons** and commanding his **disciples** to do the same. Nowadays, the signs that a person might be possessed include unusual physical strength and a severe aversion to God, the Virgin Mary, and images of the Christian faith, such as the cross.

E

35 The Church reports that only one in 5,000 cases of possession are genuine. In most instances, they find that people are mentally or physically ill. When an exorcism does take place, it involves a series of prayers asking God to free the possessed person of the devil and a set of commands ordering the devil to leave. The priest also 40 sprinkles holy water on any attendees present and makes the sign of the cross. He will also use a **relic** to touch the subject to drive evil away.

F

Many people, including Christians, find it hard to reconcile rational thinking with notions of demonic possession. There is steady 45 reportage of people being killed by the violent techniques of a growing number of so-called professional exorcists, assisted by well-meaning family members who have gone along with their orders. Victims have been beaten, drowned, suffocated, and **strangled**.

G

In some cases, the victims may have been suffering from 50 undiagnosed psychological disorders. Tourette's Syndrome makes people use offensive language and may bring on involuntary movements. And it was schizophrenia that the Romanian nun was suffering from, according to a psychiatrist who had treated her before she'd entered the convent, causing her to hear voices in 55 her head and have hallucinations. Epileptics suffering convulsions have also been exorcised in the past, as people believed this kind of violent shaking was evidence of an evil spirit.

H

The Roman Catholic Church does not have a monopoly on exorcism, however. In the United States, televised live exorcisms 60 are carried out simultaneously on audience members, and even whole families, by unofficial 'celebrity' exorcists. The 'cured' are encouraged to make donations, and most do, making this kind of 'religious venture' extremely profitable. So, if there's a demon you want to get rid of, you can choose whether to go public and pay for 65 it, or go private and get a priest to do it for free.

RECOGNIZING THE PURPOSE OF THE TEXT

What is the overall purpose of this text?

1 To demonstrate how religion and science are incompatible.

2 To suggest which forms of exorcism may be the most harmful.

3 To give a general overview of exorcism in practice today.

SCANNING 2 **In which paragraph (A–H) can you find ...**

1 the suggestion that the number of fatal exorcisms is increasing?

2 reasons why people are mistakenly believed to be possessed?

3 the description of a fictional exorcism?

4 the financial gain that can be made from performing exorcism?

5 a description of the way priests carry out exorcisms?

6 examples of behaviour that would indicate possession to a priest?

7 an exorcism which resulted in criminal charges?

8 a view that exorcism helps the spirit possessing a person's body?

RECOGNIZING KEY WORDS AND MAIN IDEAS **Complete the table using words from the text. Use no more than two words for each gap.**

Roman Catholicism	Other faiths	Anti-exorcism opinion
History Exorcism of (1) _____ mentioned in Bible. **Evidence of possession** Subject has strong dislike of religious objects like (2) _____, as well as of God and the Virgin Mary. **Ritual** • (3) _____ recited to God • (4) _____ sprinkled over observers • sign of cross • (5) _____ used at final stage	Exorcism goes back to (6) _____. Only in (7) _____ does exorcism benefit the person (8)_____.	Believers in (9) _____ cannot accept idea of possession by evil spirits. Some exorcists use (10) _____ and get families to help. Subjects could have (11) _____ such as schizophrenia. TV exorcists perform ritual exorcisms in return for (12) _____.

DISCUSSION **Discuss the questions with a partner.**

1 Should the Romanian priest have faced charges of murder? Why?/Why not?

2 Apart from reasons of physical or mental illness, what other factors may explain a person claiming to be possessed or being accused of being possessed?

3 Do you know of any other rituals which are supposed to heal, cure, or protect people?

10 Nature

PRE-READING 1 **Before you read the text, answer the questions.**

1 Most tigers living in the wild are found in (*choose 3*)

    a China.   **b** Europe.   **c** Russia.   **d** India.

2 The number of tigers living in a natural habitat is probably less than

    a 3,000.   **b** 5,000.   **c** 10,000.   **d** 15,000.

3 Tigers are mainly hunted (*choose 2*)

    a for medicinal purposes.

    b to protect livestock.

    c for export as exotic pets.

    d by rich foreigners who want a trophy.

PRE-READING 2 **Match a person (1–4) to a definition (a–d). Find the words in the text to help you.**

1 conservationist (line 4)

2 poacher (line 9)

3 middle man (line 12)

4 logger (line 24)

a A person who buys things from producers/suppliers and sells them to customers at a profit

b Someone who works to protect the environment or animals from damage or destruction

c Someone who cuts down trees to sell the wood

d Someone who illegally catches or kills animals, birds, or fish

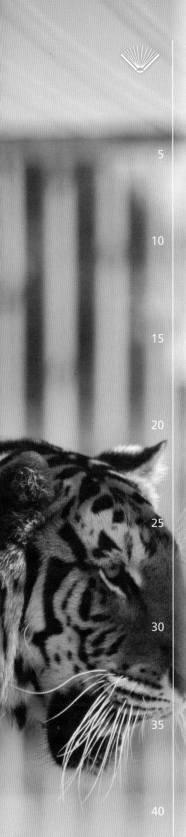

The tragedy of the tiger

Where do tigers live? North-eastern China, the Indian subcontinent, and the Russian Far East are all home to different species of this beautiful big cat, but maybe not for much longer. According to a recent study by **leading** conservationists, the wild tiger is now closer to extinction than previously realized. In fact, it is thought that there are fewer than 5,000 tigers existing in the wild around the world. Illegal hunting is a huge factor. Most countries have laws that **prohibit** the hunting and trade of these animals, but the temptation for local poachers is great. A poor villager can earn up to 60 times his daily earnings by **trapping** and killing one tiger. This money may guarantee the survival of his family. The dead tiger is handed over to a middle man, who then often smuggles it abroad. Its fur may end up hanging on a wall and its bones may be used for medicinal purposes.

The other factor affecting the survival of the wild tiger is the reduction of their natural habitat. When man moves into an area that was previously tiger territory, the tiger loses its natural prey since the villagers often hunt such animals for their own food. Then the tiger goes after the villagers' cows and goats, and so it becomes the hunted. Another problem with reduced habitat is that the tigers will not cross open land, so they cannot get to **isolated** areas of forest to breed with other tigers.

One country that has taken action over the competition for habitat is Russia. The **ancient** forests of Southern Siberia are being logged for their increasingly expensive timber. These loggers, along with the poaching of tigers and their prey, have posed a serious threat to the survival of the tiger population. However, since 1992 the Wildlife Conservation Society (WCS) has been carrying out The Siberian Tiger Project. By attaching radio collars to the tigers they can trace their movements and gather a wealth of information about their habits. In this way, the Russian government has been provided with invaluable support and advice.

The 'Tiger Response Team', a special unit of the Russian government, takes active steps towards resolving the problems between tigers and humans. One aim is to keep tigers away from human settlements. The team use fireworks or even electrified dead animals to deter the tigers from approaching villages. Sometimes the tigers are captured and simply moved to other areas. If the animal is considered too dangerous, it may be taken to a zoo on the other side of the world. At least in a protected environment like this, scientists are able to study wild tigers in a way that they could not in their natural habitat. Also, captive breeding programmes are a way to increase tiger numbers;

they can be used to introduce genetic variability into the wild tiger population.

45   The WCS also considers the management of the tigers' prey essential to the programme. This requires the establishment of large areas of habitat for both the tigers and their prey to **coexist**. This can be achieved through properly managed wildlife tourism. Tourism can generate money and jobs for local people, as well as creating

50   opportunities to conserve suitable land for tigers to live on. It is also an excellent way to educate locals and tourists in conservation issues.

There is no clear solution to saving the tiger, but there is still great pressure from

55   conservation societies and environmental groups to ensure its survival. We will only be able to do this if we can find a balance between the need of people to earn a living with the need to preserve the tigers' habitat.

COMPREHENSION 1   **Read the first paragraph of the text. Find the answers to Pre-Reading 1.**

COMPREHENSION 2   **Complete the summary with words from the text. Use no more than three words for each gap.**

One of the threats to the survival of the wild tiger is (**1**)_____, although it is hard to put the blame on the poor people who do this. (**2**)_____ is another threat to their survival. Tigers are trapped in small areas of forest and there is no longer any (**3**)_____ for them to hunt. Various solutions have been suggested. People have been studying the tigers' habits so that they can help (**4**)_____ between people and the tigers. Sometimes tigers are caught and taken to zoos, where they are used in breeding programmes to introduce (**5**)_____ into the wild tiger population. Wildlife tourism can generate (**6**)_____ for local people and is also useful in helping to (**7**)_____ and tourists. While there are still a lot of problems between tigers and humans, there are a lot of people who are working hard to save these rare animals (**8**)_____.

COMPREHENSION 3   **Answer the questions.**

1   In lines 8-9, what does the *temptation for local poachers is great* mean?

   Local poachers want to illegally trap the tigers due to ...

   a   the food the animals can provide.

   b   the respect they can earn from their community.

   c   the money they can earn from selling the animals.

2   In line 12, what is the meaning of the phrasal verb *end up*?

   a   The fur may be hung on a wall upside down.

   b   The fur may fall to pieces after it has been hanging for a while.

   c   The final destination for the fur is to be hung on a wall.

3   In lines 18-19, what does the phrase *so it becomes the hunted* mean?

   a   The tiger has to eat cows and goats instead of its usual food.

   b   The villagers begin to hunt the tiger.

   c   The tiger is forced to change its behaviour.

4   In line 41, *natural habitat* means ...

   a   a man-made home.

   b   a large landscaped zoo.

   c   an area that an animal lives in.

5   In line 41, what does *captive breeding programmes* mean?

   a   Introducing captive animals into the wild

   b   Encouraging captive animals to mate in a controlled environment

   c   Teaching captive animals how to survive in the wild

6   In line 52, what is the best definition of *conservation issues*?

   a   How to save money

   b   How to take care of animals

   c   How to protect wildlife and natural resources

VOCABULARY   **Match a word in bold in the text with a synonym below.**
SKILLS 1

1   to catch =   _____

2   live in the same place =   _____

3   very old =   _____

4   remote/far away =   _____

5   most important =   _____

6   to ban =   _____

VOCABULARY   **Use the words in Vocabulary skills 1 to complete the**
SKILLS 2   **sentences. You need to change the form of some words.**

1   It is _____ to chew gum anywhere in Singapore.

2   It's often very difficult for wild animals and people to _____ in the same area.

3   Jane Harris is a _____ spokeswoman for animal rights.

4   The researchers felt very _____ while they were living in the jungle.

5   The zoo-keepers had to set a _____ for the escaped bear.

6   _____ forests should be protected by law to prevent loggers from moving in.

Grammar

The passive

The passive is often used:
a when the receiver of the action is more important than the performer (person/group/organization).
b when the performer of the action is not someone specific.
c to avoid saying who is responsible or who is to blame for something.
d with certain verbs of saying and believing (*say/think/believe/know/estimate/consider*).

GRAMMAR 1   **Find and <u>underline</u> the following forms of the passive in the text.**

1   two examples of the present simple passive

   Line: _____   Line: _____

2   one example of the present continuous passive

   Line: _____

3   one example of the past simple passive

   Line: _____

4   one example of the present perfect passive

   Line: _____

5   four examples of a modal verb + *be* + participle

   Line: _____   Line: _____   Line: _____   Line: _____

6   one verb of saying and believing + *be* + participle

   Line: _____

GRAMMAR 2   **Put the sentences into the passive. Use the correct tense, modal verb, or verb of saying and believing.**

1   Until the late 19th century, wolves _____ (see) across Europe.

2   It is still the case that elephants _____ (hunt) for their ivory.

3   There are, it _____ (think), less than 5,000 tigers in the wild.

4   A large number of dolphins _____ (catch) in fishing nets last year.

5   Fortunately, the escaped lions _____ (just recapture).

6   When we arrived at the zoo, we _____ (inform) that the pandas _____ (transfer) to a reserve.

7   Unfortunately, this type of eagle can only _____ (see) in zoos nowadays.

8   The oldest living animal in the world _____ (believe) to be a giant turtle called Harriet.

SPEAKING   **Discuss the questions with a partner.**

1   Do you think big business is more or less important than wild animals? Why?

2   How can poaching be prevented?

3   Are zoos and wildlife conservation areas a good thing?

4   Are there any other animals you think need protection?

Should people be allowed to own exotic pets?

Effective • *Skills*

Complete the text below with the words in the box. Use a dictionary to help you.

speed	transport	pesticides	resource
fuel	pollution	organic	vehicles

The United States has the greatest number of private (**1**)_____ in the world as not many people use public (**2**)_____. Cars are responsible for a huge amount of air (**3**)_____ and in cities such as Los Angeles it can be hard to breathe. Many Americans drive SUVs and these require a lot of (**4**)_____, even when they are travelling at low (**5**)_____. This is a natural (**6**)_____ we cannot replace. On the other hand, in other areas many Americans are very health-conscious and buy (**7**)_____ food which has not been sprayed with (**8**)_____.

Read the article on page 111 quickly and answer the questions. Do not worry about unknown words.

1   What is the purpose of this text?

   a   To persuade people to be greener in their everyday lives.

   b   To highlight the consequences of not looking after the environment.

   c   To show that some people take environmental problems too seriously.

2   How would you describe the author's tone in this article?

   a   amused

   b   optimistic

   c   critical

How green *are you?*

by
Debbie Vines

What are you doing while reading this? Sipping a machine-brewed coffee from a paper cup or munching on an apple that came individually wrapped in plastic? Did you really need to use your private vehicle this morning, or is public transport just too much effort? Most of us would like to think of ourselves

5   as reasonably green, but are we really trying hard enough? For a start, do you recycle 100 per cent of your waste paper, or just the occasional newspaper when you remember? Do you think about the water you're using while brushing your teeth, or does half a tank go down the sink? Do you check the labels on your fruit and vegetables to see how much fuel it took to get them to the supermarket, or

10   do you just pick up whatever looks nice? Drivers tend to be the worst offenders. Did you know that by reducing your speed from about 62mph to 60mph you can drastically save the amount of fuel you use? And is it really that difficult to turn off the lights when you leave the room? The simplest things can make such a difference.

15   ## Email A

'I know it's economical, but I have meetings with clients to go to, and quite frequently it can take half the day to get there, so you haven't got time to admire the scenery! And if you do slow down, you just annoy the person behind you. It's stressful enough, without having people swearing at you and

20   getting too close. In theory, it's a good idea. In reality, it doesn't work.'

Email B

'I don't think we have a choice. We owe it to future generations to preserve our forests. It doesn't require much effort – you just put it all in a box and put it outside for collection once a week. But businesses are the most serious

25   offenders. Their waste paper just ends up in the bin. They should donate some of their profits to a forest-regeneration scheme.'

Email C

'This is part of a project that the children at our primary school do. They learn all about where it comes from and what happens to it when it leaves the house.

30   They also learn about pollution and how we need to stop it from harming our precious natural resources. We hope that by showing the children some small steps they can take, for instance turning off the tap, they can pass this on to their parents.'

Email D

35   'I'd love to know if your journalist, Ms Vines, practises what she preaches. She wants us to buy from local farmers, but the reality is that people simply can't afford it. And do busy housewives have time to check where their shopping comes from? I strongly doubt it. The fact is that if our farmers dropped their prices, we could buy home-grown stuff. I suspect the well-paid Ms Vines

40   only buys organic, but the rest of us have to wash off pesticides!'

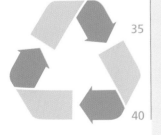

RECOGNIZING KEY VOCABULARY

Which points (1–7) are discussed in the emails?

Email A = _____   Email C = _____

Email B = _____   Email D = _____

1 food and drink packaging

2 using a private vehicle rather than public transport

3 recycling paper

4 saving water

5 buying imported produce

6 reducing speed

7 saving electricity

UNDERSTANDING DISCOURSE FEATURES

What do the examples of *it* in the emails refer to?

1 Email A

    a *it*'s economical   _____   **c** *it*'s a good idea _____

    b *It*'s stressful enough _____   **d** *it* doesn't work _____

2 Email B

    a *It* doesn't require much effort _____

    b put *it* all in a box and put *it* outside for collection _____

3 Email C

    a They learn all about where *it* comes from and what happens to *it*. _____

    b when *it* leaves the house _____

    c how we need to stop *it* from _____

4 Email D

    a She wants us to buy from local farmers, but the reality is that people simply can't afford *it*. _____

    b I strongly doubt *it*. _____

UNDERSTANDING ATTITUDE AND OPINION

Decide if the information about the text is True (T), False (F), or Not Given (NG). Write T, F, or NG.

1 (Email A) I have to drive long distances as part of my job. ☐

2 (Email A) In my experience, driving is a way of relaxing. ☐

3 (Email A) It's annoying when drivers suddenly change lanes. ☐

4 (Email B) It should be easier for householders to recycle paper. ☐

5 (Email B) Companies are worse than householders at recycling paper. ☐

6 (Email C) Parents are not well informed about environmental issues. ☐

7 (Email D) Consumers pay less for produce that comes from overseas. ☐

8 (Email D) I don't eat food that has been sprayed with chemicals. ☐

DISCUSSION **Discuss the questions with a partner.**

1 Have you recycled anything or used any recycled products this week?

2 How do you usually get to college/university?

3 Do you save water or energy in any way?

4 Do you ever make green choices when you buy or eat food?

PRONUNCIATION **When people talk at normal speed in English, their words often become linked together.**

a The *t* or *d* at the end of a word becomes silent when the next word starts with a consonant.
b Consonants at the end of a word link on to the next word when the next word starts with a vowel.
c Words that end in *y* are followed by an extra /j/ sound when the next word starts with a vowel.
d Words that end in a vowel sound are followed by an extra /w/ sound when the next word starts with a vowel.

Find examples of linking in the sentences below.

1 I know it's economical, but I have meetings to get to.

2 I can't turn up late.

3 When you're in the fast lane, people get really angry.

4 In theory, it's a good idea.

Survival tips for the North American Wilderness

What to do when you're lost

First of all, stay where you are. There's no point expending energy if you're uncertain which direction to take. Before you set off, make sure you notify someone where you're going, your intended route, and anticipated time of return, so if you *do* get lost, at least you know a rescue party is on its way. Remain calm. Your priority is to find water and shelter. You can do without food for up to a month, but dehydration will kill you after four days, and hypothermia can take just 24 hours. Look for shelter in a cave or under a fir tree, but avoid very tall trees as they can attract lightning. If you do need to eat, avoid plants as some can be quite poisonous. You're better off eating lizards, frogs, and insects.

What to do if you meet a bear

Don't turn your back and run. You will be behaving just like the bear's regular prey and it will chase you. Bears can also reach speeds of nearly 19 mph, so you have no chance of outrunning it! Heading up a tree is also inadvisable. Black bears are excellent climbers and brown bears may be capable of pushing your escape route over. Instead, look a bear firmly in the eyes and back away slowly. Drop any food you have as a bear will go after anything edible. As you move away, the bear will hopefully wander off, but if it *does* attack, most experts suggest that you play dead, so that the bear loses interest.

What to do if a snake bites you

Whatever you may have seen in films, do not attempt to suck the poison out as you will simply absorb more venom into your system. The best thing to do is to wash the affected area with soap and water, and leave a damp cloth over it. Remain still and make sure the bite point is lower than your heart. Don't panic, as this will pump the venom round your body faster. If you have a mobile phone, call for medical attention or get someone to seek help.

EXERCISE 1

Guess if the sentences are True or False. Then read the text to check.

1   If you get lost, you should keep moving and looking for a way out.

2   It is more important to find a source of food than a source of water.

3   It is more dangerous to get wet and cold than to become very thirsty.

4   You should not make shelters under tall trees.

5   Frogs are a safer source of food than plants.

6   Trees are a safe place to get away from bears.

7   It is better to pretend to be dead than to run away from a bear.

8   If a snake bites you, suck out the poison immediately.

9   You should clean a snake bite with soap.

10   The bitten part of the body should be kept higher than your heart.

EXERCISE 1

Read the text.

Beloved pets

When a loved one passes away, it can be hard to accept they are truly gone for ever, and for some, the loved ones are of the furry, four-legged variety. Some animal lovers are content with a private burial in the garden, others may want something a little more ceremonial and prefer a service at a pet cemetery. In the last decade, another option has become available, that of freeze-drying. This process involves the complete removal of liquid from a pet, so that it retains its shape and size. This can take up to four months to complete, depending on the pet's weight. It is then sent back to the owner. Initially, this service was mainly available in the United States. Now, Britain has joined the trend in pet preservation, but in the form of taxidermy. In fact, the resurrection of interest in this form of preservation is so great that the few taxidermists still practising cannot cope with demand. For the layperson, taxidermy means 'stuffing dead animals' and brings to mind dusty collections of exotic creatures in museums. For the professional taxidermist, theirs is an art form that also requires a genuine interest in wildlife. When they begin work on a subject, they must not only sculpt a body from wood or, in the case of large animals, fibreglass (the animal's skin is then stretched over this frame), but they must position the animal in a convincing pose, and they can only do this by knowing how it moved in life. The subjects, by the way, have all met natural deaths or been killed in road accidents, as British law prevents endangered species from reaching the taxidermist's table.

EXERCISE 2

Answer the question.

What is the main point of the text?

a To suggest that some people take their relationship with their pets too seriously.

b To make people reconsider their definition of art and what it includes.

c To show how a technique for preserving dead animals has become popular again.

EXERCISE 3

Complete the sentences with one or two words from the text.

1 The _____ in an animal is taken out during freeze-drying.

2 An animal's _____ affects the amount of time it takes to freeze-dry.

3 Big frames are made out of _____.

4 Taxidermists are not allowed to work on _____.

11 · Technology

PRE-READING **Before you read the text, answer the questions.**

Which of these examples of modern technology have you seen or used in the last 24 hours?

- [ ] a credit card
- [ ] a mobile phone
- [ ] a GPS
- [ ] a surveillance camera

Which of these methods (if any) do you use to gain access to a building or department?

- [ ] an iris scan
- [ ] your fingerprints
- [ ] voice recognition
- [ ] an ID card

Put these social issues in order from 1–4. (1 = the most worrying; 4 = the least worrying)

- [ ] social security fraud
- [ ] illegal immigration
- [ ] health tourism
- [ ] terrorism

Which of these crimes should be punishable by a fine (F) or by prison (P)?

- [ ] a sexual offence
- [ ] hacking into a database
- [ ] speeding
- [ ] tax evasion

Big Brother is getting bigger

A Think of an item you would never leave home without. For many people, that would be a credit card. There's no doubt that this makes any financial transaction swift and convenient, but that's not all there is to it. Whenever you use your credit card, you are creating a trail of purchasing preferences. It's already the case that most national banks will pass this information on to private companies who can then interrupt your evening with an unwelcome phone call or fill your mail box with **unsolicited** advertising in an attempt to sell their own products.

B Perhaps you were looking forward to the day when cash becomes **obsolete**. That day may also herald the credit card that limits your consumer options. If the government, for instance, wishes to reduce the budget for health care, that little microchip may not let you buy cigarettes if your family has a history of cancer. Anyone at risk of heart disease may find they can only buy low-fat, low-sugar products at the supermarket. This may sound a little **far-fetched**, but bear in mind how technology has already invaded your privacy. Your mobile phone can tell a GPS exactly where you are and surveillance cameras can record your entire day's movements.

C At the moment, the citizens of many countries carry identity cards. These bear a photograph of the owner's face, information about their date of birth, social security number, and signature, and it is not compulsory to carry them on you. However, this may all be about to change with the introduction of the biometric card.

D Biometric cards are already used in institutions that require a high level of security, such as nuclear facilities or national banks. The microchips on the cards contain the employees' physiological data, such as an iris scan or their fingerprints. Some operate through voice recognition. The United States is also testing a Registered Traveler Program, in which frequent, usually affluent, fliers can use a biometric card to breeze through airport security, while ordinary people remain under suspicion and in a long queue for a security check. But now, some countries are **contemplating** the **deployment** of the card on a much greater scale. Britain is so far leading the way. The current government hopes that by 2013 the Passport Office will have issued biometric cards to most British citizens and legal residents. At this stage, the government will vote on whether to make it compulsory to carry one.

E The government initially proposed the cards as a means of combating social security fraud. Now, they insist the cards are essential to prevent illegal immigration, health tourism and terrorism. In addition to containing physiological data, the microchip will store details such as every address you've ever had. This information will also be held in a central database, the National Identity Register, and will be available to the police, government departments, the Inland Revenue, and Immigration and Intelligence services. It will also be available to certain private companies, although the government has not made it clear exactly which ones will have this privilege.

F The government has yet to vote on whether a DNA sample should be part of the data – and this is one of the issues that most concerns human rights groups and civil libertarians. Until recently, only sex offenders and murderers had to provide DNA samples, but now countries such as the United States, the UK, Germany and Canada require samples after any arrestable offence, including speeding.

G At the moment, you might think none of this sounds too bad, but what happens if all your personal information, all stored on one card and in one database, falls into the wrong hands? For a start, imagine that someone hacks into your profile. Within an hour, your identity has been stolen and someone is using a passport under your name. Imagine a face from the past has a personal **vendetta** against you and now works in a government department. After a short time on the keyboard, he or she could seriously ruin up your life by adding a few convictions for theft and tax evasion. Imagine that you're not ill, but that an analysis of your DNA suggests you might be someday, so you can't get insurance or any kind of loan from a bank.

H And one of the worst-case scenarios? Some governments have used compulsory card-carrying programmes to discriminate against people of different races and religions. How do you know what the government will be doing with biometric cards ten years from now? If you've ever felt lonely living in a big city – don't. A lot of people out there already know all about you!

COMPREHENSION 1 **Which paragraph in the text (A–H) contains this information? <u>Underline</u> the keywords in the text.**

1 Details of what physiological data may be contained on biometric cards in the future. Paragraph: _____

2 Examples of how the government could control the way you spend your money. Paragraph: _____

3 Examples of how your biometric data could be used for criminal purposes. Paragraph: _____

4 A description of a widely-used means of voluntary identification. Paragraph: _____

5 Examples of how biometric cards are already in use. Paragraph: _____

6 An explanation of which groups may legally access your biometric data. Paragraph: _____

7 An explanation of how certain companies have access to your spending patterns. Paragraph: _____

8 Examples of how modern technology can reveal your location. Paragraph: _____

COMPREHENSION 2 **Answer the questions.**

1 In lines 3–4, what is meant by *that's not all there is to it*?

   a Using a credit card is not swift and convenient all of the time.

   b We need to consider the disadvantages of using a credit card.

   c People use a credit card for a variety of reasons.

2 In lines 4–5, how can you rewrite *you are creating a trail of purchasing preferences?*

   a It is possible for someone to see what things you like to buy.

   b You owe more and more money to your credit card company.

   c Using a credit card is always your first choice, rather than cash.

3 In lines 31–33, what is meant by *while ordinary people remain under suspicion and in a long queue for a security check*?

   a It is normal-looking people who have something to hide.

   b Travellers without biometric cards will be treated cautiously.

   c It will be a long time before security becomes less strict at airports.

4 In lines 34–35, how can you rewrite *Britain is so far leading the way*?

   Britain is ...

   a telling other countries that they must also use biometric cards.

   b starting to introduce biometric cards before other countries.

   c finding out whether people want biometric cards or not.

5 In line 50, what is the meaning of *The government has yet to vote*?

The government ...

   a   has recently voted.

   b   will vote in the future.

   c   voted some time ago.

6 In lines 58–59, what is another way of saying *your personal information ... falls into the wrong hands?*

Your personal information ...

   a   becomes part of someone else's biometric data.

   b   is recorded by someone who makes errors with details.

   c   is found by someone who uses it in a way that benefits them and harms you.

7 In line 62, why does the writer use *a face from the past?*

He wants to suggest ...

   a   it often takes time for someone to plan their revenge.

   b   your biometric data is available to anyone who wants it.

   c   you will not be aware of who is trying to cause you problems.

8 In line 69, what is meant by *one of the worst-case scenarios?*

One of the worst situations ...

   a   we can imagine.

   b   that has already happened.

   c   that could possibly happen.

VOCABULARY SKILLS 1   **Match the words in bold in the text to a definition below Check your answers in a dictionary.**

1 _____ = Difficult to believe because it is very unlikely

2 _____ = To consider doing something in future

3 _____ = A situation in which someone has angry/negative feelings towards someone else and keeps trying to harm or cause problems for them

4 _____ = The use of something (*formal*)

5 _____ = Not required/not asked for

6 _____ = No longer used because it has been replaced by something newer and more effective

To consider doing something in future

VOCABULARY SKILLS 2

Use the correct form of the words in bold to complete the sentences.

1   Do you agree that biometric cards are an _____ of privacy? **invade**

2   Will taxes be raised in order to _____ this new scheme? **financial**

3   We can arrange the meeting at your _____. **convenient**

4   It's almost impossible to _____ the police if they use GPS. **evasion**

5   The use of credit cards has resulted in uncontrolled _____. **consumer**

6   Plastic surgery could make some criminals _____. **recognition**

Grammar

Future forms

*How do you know what the government **will be using** biometric cards for ten years from now?*

This sentence refers to a future point in time (*ten years from now*). It suggests that the government will start using biometric cards for a new purpose before the ten-year point, and will continue after the ten-year point.

*By 2013, the Passport Office **will have issued** biometric cards to most British citizens.*

This sentence refers to a future time (2013). It suggests that the action of issuing biometric cards will be completed sometime before this point.

GRAMMAR

Choose the most appropriate future form.

1   This time tomorrow, we'll *be flying / have flown* halfway to our destination.

2   In the next decade, many people will *be living / have lived* in solar-powered homes.

3   Robots will *be replacing / have replaced* all the manual workers in this section by 2020.

4   Scientists will *be finding / have found* a way to stop ageing by the end of the next century.

5   Let's hope that the government will *be changing / have changed* its mind about biometric cards by 2013.

6   I doubt I'll still *be working / have worked* in this department when the new management takes over.

SPEAKING

Discuss the questions with a partner.

1   Do you think using biometric cards will create advantages or disadvantages for people?

2   Which three items of technology do you use every day? In what ways might these items of technology invade your privacy?

Effective • *Skills*

ACTIVATING VOCABULARY

Use your dictionary to translate the sets of words.

1 rhythm = _____   improvisation = _____

   music track = _____   composition = _____

2 gig = _____   performance = _____

   front-line act = _____ cultural event = _____

Describe the following people: guess what they do and what they are like.

3 a promoter   a member of the arts crowd   a party person

Use one word from each set 1-3 above to complete the sentences.

a A lot of musicians are afraid of _____. They feel more comfortable if they can practise first.

b Almost every musician wants to be a _____.

c One _____ I knew always booked three bands for every gig because he knew two would never arrive.

SKIMMING

Skim the text and put the following events in chronological order:

Simon …

a mostly played at clubs.

b played for people who listened carefully to his music.

c performed in Russia.

d used older technology.

e played at a very simple venue.

f started using his own computer.

1 _____   4 _____

2 _____   5 _____

3 _____   6 _____

Techno tour of Europe

It's not easy to break into the club scene in Europe but one musician who is starting to make an impression is Simon Flower. He describes his music like this: 'I would call it generally Electronic Music but inside that you've got different smaller genres, so it's a type of
5   Modern Techno or Modern House music. The sounds are all made by synthesizers. I love the crazy sounds they make and I love rhythm so putting those things together is what really excites me.'

However, Simon has changed the way he works. 'When I started making music I used real synthesizers, which meant working in a big
10   space with heavy and cumbersome equipment. These days I work almost entirely on my computer, replicating the sounds with a virtual synthesizer. On screen I can create everything in the music from scratch.'

While working on a composition he is constantly experimenting with
15   a vast array of sounds and rhythms, which he gradually combines to create the end piece that he has in mind. He then practises for hours, just as an old-fashioned rock band would, until he can recreate the correct combinations in performance. 'When I get into a club I see which parts work and which structures get the best response from the
20   crowd. If I like them, the new ideas work their way into the final track.'

There is also room for improvisation while he's performing. Because he has programmed his computer in advance to recognize what he needs for a given track, he is then able to adjust the mix of sounds spontaneously. 'If I don't like a sound I can just delete it. If I love a
25   sound I can make it do different things, depending on the situation. If I make a mistake, that's fine. It simply adds to the creative process and I see this as an essential part of producing any art.'

30

Simon's music is growing increasingly popular in Europe. When he tours, he is the front-line act. The gigs are sold on his name and he is actively sought after by promoters. Most of these gigs take place in clubs, but last year's tour was a bit different. After his first stop in Moscow, he then went to Berlin and performed at a cultural event that was paid for by The House of World Cultures. Simon was impressed.

35

'The performance was in a beautiful and elegant old building where the crowd was more of an arts crowd. Unlike a typical dance party, there was very little crowd feedback. They were very quiet and respectful, worlds apart from a normal gig.'

He then moved on to Cologne and this gig was different again. 'The promoter, a dentist with a full-time practice, organizes dance parties

40

twice a month. He staged our event in an underground concrete bunker with a temporary sound system and one static red light. It was very dark, no flashing lights and no frills. It was all very much about the music.'

This is what Simon particularly likes about touring Europe. 'Every

45

promoter I've ever met has been hard-working and passionate about creating a great party. They aren't the stereotypical party people who are only there to see and be seen. They are people who are serious about the music they love, and they work hard to achieve the highest quality possible', he says.

UNDERSTANDING PURPOSE, ATTITUDE AND OPINION

Answer the questions.

1 In paragraph 2, Simon compares the present with the past. He says that …

   a in the past he made all the music himself.

   b his music is now better than before.

   c the instrument he uses today is more compact than when he began.

2 If Simon makes mistakes when he is performing, he doesn't mind because …

   a he can change it immediately.

   b it helps him to improve his music.

   c other people might like his mistakes.

3 Simon's Berlin gig was unusual because the audience …

   a responded differently.

   b was made up of artists.

   c didn't like his music.

4 In the last paragraph, Simon uses the expression *only there to see and be seen* to suggest that some promoters …

    a think it is important for musicians to look good.

    b are more interested in socialising than the music.

    c watch the musicians carefully to make sure they work hard.

VOCABULARY EXTENSION   **Guess the meaning of these phrases and write a translation. Compare your ideas with a partner.**

1 from scratch   _____

2 vast array   _____

3 the creative process   _____

4 actively sought after   _____

In what other situations might you …

5 start something from scratch?

6 use a vast array of something?

7 experience the creative process?

8 be actively sought after?

DISCUSSION   **Discuss the questions with a partner.**

1 Do you enjoy listening to electronic music? Why/Why not?

2 Do you think that going to live gigs has any negative effects?

3 Do you think that modern musicians make good role models for young people?

4 If you could excel in any kind of artistic field, which would it be?

12 • 21st-century love

PRE-READING 1 **Use your dictionary to find a translation for the three words in each set. Then choose the correct word to complete the sentences.**

1 **a** soulmate **b** feminist **c** guru

Sarah is well-known as a leading fitness _____, but people also seek her advice about their spiritual well-being.

2 **a** seduction **b** exploitation **c** manipulation

The government wants to introduce a law to stop the _____ of children by companies. At the moment, companies pay them a very low wage for very long hours.

3 **a** to compliment s.o. **b** to insult s.o. **c** to trick s.o.

My boss _____ me on the presentation that I gave to our clients from Berlin, so I hope I get a bonus next month!

4 **a** sequel **b** biography **c** manual

Young people seem to understand new technology instinctively. Older people prefer to read a _____ before they operate anything.

PRE-READING 2 **You are going to read a text about two books giving advice on dating. Decide if these statements are from a book giving advice about dating for women (W) or for men (M).**

1 You must not offer to pay when you eat out on a date. _____

2 End the relationship if the other person doesn't remember special occasions. _____

3 Don't make it too easy for the other person to have a date with you. _____

4 Don't respond every time the other person leaves a message. _____

5 Listen carefully and show interest when your partner is speaking. _____

6 Show a lot of interest when you first meet and then ignore the other person. _____

Words of love?

'Have you read it?' Lily asks me excitedly. I shake my head and she passes it over. The coffee shop is filling up with students after the last lecture and more girls are coming to join us with the same book in their hands. It's not a textbook. It's the latest manual on how to get the perfect man. At this time in our lives, that can feel a lot more difficult than getting the perfect score in our tests.

If you're a player in the dating game, you'll know it can be a minefield of potential embarrassments, disasters, and regrets. It's no wonder that people seek advice. Go to your local bookshop or online and you will find an incredible range of self-help books. All of them claim to have the answers. While we were living in New York, my sister Madeline, **got hold of** a signed copy of *The Rules: Time-Tested Secrets for Capturing the Heart of Mr. Right* by Ellen Fein and Sherrie Schneider. It first came out in 1995 and has been translated into 27 languages, from Korean and Croatian to Icelandic and Italian (surely the Italians don't need any help!).

For women who couldn't get a second or even a first date with a guy, *The Rules* became a kind of sacred text. It told them to play hard-to-get, and that no man could resist a challenge. They should listen attentively and look at him demurely, but only see him once a week. He had to phone or email them four times before they replied. They should never split the bill at a restaurant and should stop **going out with** him as soon as he forgot an event that was significant, such as a birthday or anniversary.

The response from men was that the book was all about manipulation: a way of tricking them into marriage. And not all women were impressed either, finding it highly patronizing. My sister briefly considered becoming a 'Rules Facilitator' to help spread the message when we got back to the UK, but decided to spend more time with her new boyfriend instead. I don't know if Madeline got her man because of *The Rules*, or despite it, and I'm not sure if I'd borrow it from Lily. After all, Ellen Fein's marriage **broke up** just as the sequel *The Rules for Marriage* **came out**.

I think a lot of men would find that funny, including my brother, Ken. For him, the outcome of a date isn't marriage. It's just more dates, and maybe the chance to **check out** the current date's friends. Unfortunately for Ken, he's a bit nervous with most women. He's tried following the advice of one of those online dating-advice gurus, but to no avail. But recently a cousin in the

40 | United States sent him a book called *The Game* and his head has
been stuck in the pages ever since.

After some Internet research, I discovered that *The Game* seems to be
the literary nemesis of *The Rules*. Author Neil Strauss, a writer for
Rolling Stone magazine, wrote this autobiographical book after two
45 | years perfecting his seduction techniques under the guidance of a
man called 'Mystery.' Strauss claims to be able to impress any
woman by using a variety of mind games, including a technique he
refers to as 'negging.' It's a way of complimenting and insulting a
woman at the same time, for instance: 'I like your hair. A lot of
50 | women have that style, don't they?' According to Strauss, this makes
the woman feel insecure and more likely to respond gratefully to
any positive attention he might give her.

Another technique would be to look deeply into a woman's eyes
and warmly squeeze her hand while being introduced, and then
55 | suddenly turn away and talk to someone else, preferably female.
That would be enough bait to get the first woman hooked. *The Game*
has been the target of a lot of anger from feminists, who see it as an
inhuman way of treating another human being. But it was also at
the top of the *New York Times* bestseller list for months. Well, I still
60 | can't help thinking that Ken might make more progress with
women if he showed he was trying to get a full-time job!

I'm the first to admit that I'm not an expert in human psychology,
but it seems to me that our confusion over what we should be
looking for (from soulmate to one-night-stand) and how to achieve
65 | it (through playing hard-to-get to playing mind games) has made us
vulnerable to commercial exploitation. I know it's more complicated
than this, but I'm sure that if you can put pen to paper, you can
make a great deal of money out of people seeking that elusive
perfect relationship, or who lack the self-confidence to talk to the
70 | opposite sex.

When you stop to think about it, Lily and Ken are in the same boat
(although it's easier for men – you can go on dates and your parents
don't give you a hard time!). No matter what they might be reading
right now, they both still want to get married and they obviously
75 | want to make the right choice. As for me, I can't pretend I'm
disinterested. I think I've got another six or seven years to go until
my parents start to worry and put pressure on me. The difference is, I
just don't want to pay someone to tell me how to find my soulmate!
Just think – my grandparents have been happily married for over 50
80 | years, and I'm sure they didn't have self-help books in their day.
Maybe it's time I gave Grandma a call!

COMPREHENSION 1   **Answer the questions.**

1   What can we conclude about the writer's opinion of self-help books?

   a   Writers of self-help books are making money from people's uncertainty about relationships.

   b   Women are more likely than men to believe that self-help books can improve their lives in some way.

2   What can we conclude about the writer's opinion of marriage?

   a   She believes that marriage was more important to the older generation.

   b   She hopes that she will get married to the right person in the future.

COMPREHENSION 2   **Find the correct answers to the statements in Pre-Reading 2. Write line numbers next to each statement to show where you found the answers.**

COMPREHENSION 3   **Answer the questions.**

1   In line 8, when the writer uses *minefield* to describe dating, she is implying that ...

   a   there are better ways than dating to meet a suitable partner.

   b   you are sure to face many unexpected problems when dating.

   c   the consequences of dating can be extremely harmful.

2   In lines 8–9, what is the function of *It's no wonder*?

   It shows that the writer ...

   a   understands   **b**   disapproves of   **c**   is confused by

   the reasons why people seek advice.

3   Which expression in lines 18–19 means *to pretend not to be interested in someone who you think is attractive in order to make them more interested in you*?

4   In line 31, what does the writer imply by using *or despite it*?

   a   Madeline ignored the advice in *The Rules*.

   b   It was surprising that Madeline found a boyfriend because she was following the advice in *The Rules*.

   c   Madeline had found a boyfriend before she read *The Rules*.

5   In line 39, what is the meaning of *to no avail*?

   a   although Ken only received negative suggestions

   b   but he found no one to practise on

   c   Ken followed their advice without success

6   In lines 40–41, how can you rewrite *his head has been stuck in the pages ever since*?

   a   Ken is fascinated by this book.

   b   Ken is trying to work out what the writer is saying.

   c   Ken has got the wrong idea about how relationships work.

7   In line 56, what is the meaning of *bait* and *hooked*?

   bait =   *hooked =*

   a   the man's behaviour   **d**   fallen in love

   b   the other woman   **e**   become fascinated with

   c   a way of holding hands   **f**   become angry with

   In this sentence, the writer is using a metaphor for ...

   g   hunting.   **h**   trapping.   **i**   fishing.

8   In lines 59–60, what is another way of saying *I still can't help thinking*?

   a   I still worry

   b   I still believe

   c   I still don't understand

9   Find an expression in lines 67–68 which means *able to write*.

10   In lines 71–72, how can you rewrite *Lily and Ken are in the same boat*?

   a   They both have few choices about who they get married to.

   b   They would be suitable partners.

   c   They are in a similar situation.

VOCABULARY SKILLS   **Use one of the phrasal verbs in bold in the text to complete the sentences. Use your dictionary to help you if necessary.**

1   It looks likely that the band will _____ if they can't agree on their musical direction.

2   Do you want to _____ that new bar in King Street? It's supposed to be great.

3   Spielberg's new film is due to _____ in Tokyo next spring.

4   I've been trying to _____ a good recipe for chocolate cake on the Internet.

5   I'm not interested in gossip columns. Who cares who is _____ who!

Grammar

Verbs with gerund or infinitive

There is a set of verbs in English which can either be followed by the gerund or the infinitive with a different meaning. For example:

a *try + -ing* shows that we test something to see if it works.
   He's **tried** follow**ing** the advice.

b *try + infinitive* shows that we attempt to do something difficult.
   He **was trying to get** a serious job.

GRAMMAR **Match the explanations (a and b) to the correct sentences.**

This is a way of admitting a mistake.

1 a this is a way of admitting a mistake
b this is a way of politely giving bad news

I regret spending all that money at the dating agency! _____
I regret to tell you that we haven't found a partner for you. _____

2 a Sue went to a club with the intention of finding her perfect man.
b Sue no longer goes to clubs to find her perfect man.

Sue stopped going to clubs to look for her perfect man. _____
Sue stopped to go to a club to look for her perfect man. _____

3 a My blind date only talked about her ex-boyfriend.
b My blind date changed the subject and began to talk about her ex-boyfriend.

My blind date went on talking about her ex-boyfriend for the whole evening. _____
After telling me about her job, my blind date went on to talk about her ex-boyfriend. _____

4 a I met my wife at a party, but I no longer have a memory of it.
b I was supposed to meet my wife at a party, but I forgot the arrangement.

I don't remember meeting my wife at that party. _____
I didn't remember to meet my wife at the party. _____

5 a this shows an intention or plan
b this shows what is required or necessary

If you want a big wedding, it'll mean saving all our money. _____
I mean to get married by the time I'm thirty! _____

6 a the speaker knows that this is a difficult thing to do
b the speaker is suggesting a possible way of finding a boyfriend

If you want to meet a nice man, try using a dating agency. _____
If you want to meet a nice man, try not to be so shy! _____

Effective • *Skills*

SKIMMING AND SCANNING 1
Read the first paragraph of the text on page 133 as quickly as possible. Answer the questions by <u>underlining</u> the relevant parts of the text.

1 Who is the advertisement aimed at?

2 What service is being advertised?

SKIMMING AND SCANNING 2
Decide whether these statements are True (T) or False (F). Read the text as quickly as possible to check your answers.

1 You can register for the dating event when you arrive at the location where it is taking place. ☐

2 Only people who are attending the dating event will be allowed in the restaurant or bar that the organizers have chosen. ☐

3 After you pay your fee to the host of the dating event, you do not have to pay for any more drinks. ☐

4 The single men and women looking for a partner are only allowed to talk to each other for five minutes. ☐

5 If you like a man or woman you meet, you should give them your contact details during the dating event. ☐

Too busy for love?

Made-in-Heaven

Who are you likely to meet at a Made-in-Heaven dating event?

Many hundreds of single people aged between 18 and 35 have already attended a special evening organized by Made-in-Heaven. Even if you don't find your soulmate, you will meet a range of interesting and professional people, often from diverse countries such as France, Italy, Australia, the Netherlands, Japan, and the United States.

How does a Made-in-Heaven speed dating event work?

Register online at www.madeinheaven.com and check our SCHEDULED EVENTS page to find a time and location that suits you. You must register in advance so we can make sure an equal number of men and women attend the event.

♥ Meet your host at a stylish private restaurant or bar that Made-in-Heaven has chosen specially for its comfortable atmosphere. Made-in-Heaven daters will have exclusive use of the venue for that evening.

♥ Once your host has received payment, you are given a complimentary drink* and a Match Sheet with the names of all your possible dates. (*normal bar charges apply after this)

♥ Women stay in their seats. The men spend five minutes with each woman until the bell rings and then they must move on to the next woman.

♥ Choose 'Yes' or 'No' for each of the names of the people you met on your Match Sheet and hand it to your host.

♥ When you get home, check your email. We will tell you if any of your 'Yes' dates also chose you.

♥ You can now receive their contact details and it's up to you to organize the next date by yourselves!

UNDERSTANDING ATTITUDE AND OPINION

Read the comments three students made about the text.

Who ...

1 really disagrees with the concept of speed dating?

2 approves of speed dating for other people?

3 would be willing to try speed dating?

A Eric

I would say that speed dating is quite interesting. It's set up for people in same social group. The daters don't have to search around for the perfect person. On the other hand, the time is too short to get to know somebody and impress somebody. Also, if you talk to more than five people in one evening, you may get too confused to even remember the name or details about the person. Speed dating is not suitable for me.

B Kay

Before I read this, I thought speed dating was for girls who need money. So I thought this was illegal. But after reading that advertisement, it seems to me that it is so good way. I can find friends or partners quickly, and most of all I can save money and time. It's nice to meet people I need to, especially for business.

C Jean-Phillippe

From my perspective, speed dating is not really the best way to network. This kind of meeting doesn't allow you to know the person who is sitting in front of you. I would prefer making friends in this way and not starting a romance. Actually, I don't want to decide which person I will be with, but I want to let destiny decide for me. Speed dating is for people who are just too busy and I don't belong to this kind of person.

ERROR CORRECTION

The students all made some small errors. Choose one of the words or phrases in bold in each sentence to improve it.

1 It's set up for **the** people in **the** same social group.

2 The time is too short to get to know somebody and impress **them/it**.

3 Speed dating **is not for me/is unlike me**.

4 I thought speed dating was for girls who need money **so I/So, I** thought this was illegal.

5 It seems to me that it is **a really good/really a good** way.

6 **I'm not included in that./I'm not like that.**

VOCABULARY EXTENSION 1 **What do the following words and phrases from the text mean?**

Word/Phrase	Synonym/Explanation	Translation
1 soulmate (*n*)		
2 diverse (*adj*)		
3 complimentary (*adj*)		
4 to hand something to someone		
5 it's up to you		

VOCABULARY EXTENSION 2 **Decide which of the collocations is not possible.**

1 My *husband/girlfriend/friend/partner* is my true soulmate.

2 A diverse range of *weather/nationalities/interests/TV programmes*.

3 A complimentary *TV channel/drink/snack on an aeroplane/newspaper*.

4 To hand someone *a book/a letter/a TV/a drink*.

UNDERSTANDING DISCOURSE FEATURES **In which of the following situations should you reply, *It's up to you*?**

1 You go to a job interview. The interviewer tells you that you have a good CV, but lots of other people also want the job.

2 An English-speaking friend invites you to the cinema and asks which film you want to see.

3 You visit an Australian friend. He asks you if you want tea or coffee.

DISCUSSION **Discuss the questions with a partner.**

1 Which of the following are usual ways to find a new boyfriend/girlfriend in your country?

- You meet in a bar
- You meet at a friend's house
- The other person is a colleague
- Your friends organize a blind date for you
- Your parents find a partner for you
- You join an online dating agency
- You go speed dating

2 Which of the ways above would you try/never try?

EXERCISE 1

Read the report as quickly as possible.

The Sonic Teenager Deterrent

If you're out with a group of people, but you're the only one who can hear an unbearable high-pitched noise and it's driving you crazy, the chances are that you're the only person under 20. And if you're out late at night and congregating around a shop or in a car park, the chances are even higher that what you're hearing is the Sonic Teenager Deterrent, a gadget specifically designed to drive young trouble makers away. Unfortunately, the Mosquito, as it's otherwise known, makes no distinction between well-behaved teens and those in gangs. The under 20s all have the capacity to hear high-frequency band widths and 90 per cent of older people do not. The Mosquito is a remote-controlled device that comes packaged in a small black box and emits bursts of pulsing sounds that are effective more than 20 yards away. It is the brainchild of Howard Stapleton, who was once an electronics apprentice at British Aerospace. Stapleton created it after becoming fed up with local youths who were intimidating customers at his local shop. His four children were his original guinea pigs, and Stapleton knew his invention worked when they clutched their ears and ran away. Now that it has been bought by hundreds of shopowners and several local authorities, the Mosquito is tormenting many other teens who are loitering in the wrong place at the wrong time.

EXERCISE 2

Underline the answers to the questions in the text.

1   What is the purpose of the Sonic Teenager Deterrent?

2   What is its other name?

3   What does it look like?

4   What does it do?

5   Who invented it and why?

6   Who did the inventor use to test the Sonic Teenager Deterrent?

EXERCISE 3

Find words that mean …

1   so extreme that you cannot deal with the pain/feeling (*adj*)

2   to gather together in a group (*v*)

3   a difference between two things

4   a machine or piece of equipment that does a particular thing

5   to send something out into the air, for example gas, sound, light, heat

6   an original idea

7   to deliberately make someone frightened or nervous

8   someone who is used in an experiment

9   to hold something firmly because you are in pain

10   to stand or wait in a public place, with the possible intention of committing a crime

Review | Unit 12

EXERCISE 1

Read the text.

Samoa

When reporting on foreign culture, the media often focus on what seems alien, and the Polynesian island of Samoa is certainly a target of this kind of reporting. Whenever a journalist comes looking for a story, they inevitably focus on the *fa'afafine* (Samoan men who dress as women) and overlook most other aspects of Samoan culture. Almost without exception, they misrepresent the valued place that a *fa'afafine* has in the community.

Fa'afafine translates as *in the manner of a woman*. In traditional Samoan society, when a family had a large number of male children, one would be selected to help his mother. The choice would be based on which son showed the most ability and interest in domestic chores, and he would then be dressed and raised as female. The choice was in no way based on the sexual preferences the family believed the son might have. It was a choice based on who was best suited to a certain kind of labour. The *fa'afafine*'s abilities in the home and in producing crafts, combined with physical strength, were a useful asset to Samoan communities. When the son grew up, he would marry and have children, as is expected of all Samoan men, but continue to retain a female identity. Modern-day Samoa has strong Christian beliefs, as well as a firm sense of cultural identity, and many Samoans resent the Western description of *fa'afafine* as homosexual.

EXERCISE 2

Decide if the sentences are True (T), False (F), or if the information is Not Given (NG) in the text.

1 Journalists tend to choose unusual things in other cultures to write about. ☐

2 Journalists prefer to avoid writing articles about the *fa'afafine* in Samoa. ☐

3 Journalists do not understand the role of the *fa'afafine* in Samoan society. ☐

4 Samoan parents choose a son to become a *fa'afafine* when they have no daughters. ☐

5 *Fa'afafine* were chosen according to their particular work skills. ☐

6 A *fa'afafine* went back to living as a man once he got married. ☐

Effective *Vocabulary*

The following are words from this book which are very common in academic settings.

Base word	Common forms	Translation/model senten
abandon	abandonment, abandoned	
academic	academically, academic (n), academy	
access	access (v), accessible	
achieve	achievable, achievement, achiever	
acquire	acquisition, acquisitive	
adapt	adaptable, adaptability, adapted, adaptation	
adult	adulthood	
advocate	advocate (v), advocacy	
alter	alternative, alternate, alteration	
analyze	analyst, analytical, analysis	
apparent	apparently	
approach	approach (v), approachable	
aspect		
assignment	assign	
assist	assistant, assistance	
attitude	attitudinal	
attribute	attribute (v), attributable, attribution	
author	authorship, authoress, authorial	
automatic	automatically	
available	availability	
aware	awareness	
beneficial	benefit, benefiting	
brief	briefly	
challenge	challenge (v), challenger, challenging	

Base word	Common forms	Translation/model sentence
chemical	chemical (adj), chemically	
classic	classical	
channel	channel (v)	
colleague		
commentator	comment, commentary	
commodity		
communication	communicate, communicative, communicatively, communicator	
community	commune	
complex	complexity	
computer	computerize, compute	
concept	conceptual, conceptualize, conceptualization, conception, conceive	
confine	confinement, confinable, confined, confining	
consistently	consistent	
consumer	consume, consumption, consumable, consumerism	
constantly	constant	
contact	contact (v), contactable	
contemporary	contemporary (adj)	
contribute	contribution, contributor, contributing, contributory	
convention	conventional, convene	
convince	convincing, convincible, convinced	
corporation	corporatism, corporate	
create	creator, creative, creativity, creation	
credit	credit (v), creditor, credit-worthy	
culture	cultural, culturally, cultured, multi-culturalism	
cycle	cyclic, cyclical	
definite	definitely	
deny	denial, deniable	

Base word	Common forms	Translation/model sentence
depression	depress, depressed, depressive, depressing	
designer	designer (adj), design	
despite		
discriminate	discrimination, discriminatory, discriminating	
distort	distortion, distorted	
diverse	diversity, diversification, diversify, diversified	
domestic	domesticity, domestication, domesticate, domesticated	
economy	economics, economist, economize, economic, economical, economically	
element	elemental	
enable	enabled, enabling	
encounter	encounter (v)	
enormous	enormity	
ensure		
environment	environmentalist, environmental, environmentally	
establish	establishment, established	
estimate	estimation, estimate (v), estimated	
ethics	ethical, ethically	
eventual	eventually, eventuality, eventuate	
evidence	evident, evidently	
evolve	evolution, evolutionary, evolving	
exceed	excess, excessive	
exclude	exclusion, exclusive, excluding, exclusively	
expert	expertise, expert (adj), expertly	
exploit	exploitation, exploiter, exploitative	
expose	exposure, exposed	
facility	facilitate	

Base word	Common forms	Translation/model sentence
fee		
final	finality, finalize, finalist, finally	
flexible	flexibility, flex	
focus	focus (v), focused, focal	
format	format (v)	
function	function (v), functional, functionally, functioning	
furthermore		
generation	generational	
global	globe, globalization, globalize, globalized	
guarantee	guarantee (v), guaranteed, guarantor	
highlight	highlights, highlight (v), highlighted	
identify	identity, identification, identifiable, identifiably	
ignore	ignored	
illustrate	illustration, illustrator, illustrative	
image	imagery	
immigration	immigrant, immigrate	
indication	indicator, indicate, indicative	
individual	individuality, individualism, individualist, individualistic, individualize, individually	
inevitable	inevitably	
infrastructure		
initial	initiate, initially	
injury	injure, injured, injurious	
instance	instant, instantly, instantaneous	
intelligence	intelligent, intelligently	
intensity	intensify, intense, intensely, intensive	
investigate	investigation, investigator, investigative	
involve	involvement, involving, involved	
isolate	isolation, isolated, isolating, isolationism	

Base word	Common forms	Translation/model sentence
issue	issue (v)	
item	itemize	
journal	journalist, journalism, journalese, journalistic	
justify	justification, justifiable, justified, justly, justice	
label	label (v), labelled	
labour	labourer, labour (v), laborious, laboured	
lecture	lecturer, lectureship, lecture (v)	
legal	legality, legalese, legalize, legalistic, legally	
liberal	liberality, liberalism, liberalize, liberated, liberal (adj)	
locate	location, localize, local, locally	
maintain	maintenance	
major		
manipulate	manipulation, manipulator, manipulative	
media		
military	militarism, militarist, militarize, militarized, militaristic	
minimum	minimalist, minimalism, minimize, minimal, minimally, minimalistic	
motivation	motivator, motivate, motivating, motivated	
network	networking, networker, network (v)	
nevertheless		
nonetheless		
notion	notional	
obvious	obviously	
occupy	occupation, occupier, occupied	
occur	occurrence	
odd	oddity, oddly	
option	opt, optional	

Base word	Common forms	Translation/model sentence
overcome		
overseas		
partner	partnership, partner (v)	
passive	passivity, passively	
per cent	percentage	
perspective		
phase	phase (v)	
phenomena	phenomenon, phenomenal, phenomenally	
physical	physically	
policy		
pose	poser	
potential	potentiality, potential (adj), potentially	
previous	previously	
primary	prime, primarily	
prior	priority, prioritize	
procedure	proceed, procedural, processed	
process	processor, processing	
professional	professional, professionalism, professionalize, professionally	
prohibit	prohibition, prohibitive, prohibited	
promote	promotion, promoter, promotional, promoted	
prospect	prospective	
psychology	psychologist, psychological, psychologically	
purchase	purchase (v), purchaser, purchased	
pursue	pursuer, pursuit, pursued	
range	range (v)	
rational	rationale, rationalize, rationalist, rationalization, rationally	
react	reaction	

Base word	Common forms	Translation/model sentence
recover	recovery, recoverable, recovered	
release	release (v), released	
relevance	relevant, relevantly	
reluctance	reluctant, reluctantly	
rely	reliance, reliable, reliably, reliant	
remove	remover, removal, removable, removed	
residence	residency, resident, reside, residential	
resource	resourced, resourceful	
require	requirement, required	
revelation	reveal, revelatory, revealing	
revenue		
reverse	reverse (v) (adj)	
revolution	revolutionary (n) (adj), revolt, revolutionize	
route		
scenario		
schedule	schedule (v), scheduled	
section	sectional	
security	secure (v) (adj)	
seek	seeker	
select	selection, selector, selected, selective, selectively	
series	serial	
significance	signification, signify, significant, significantly	
similarity	similar, similarly	
sole	solely	
source	source (v)	
specification	specify, specific, specifically	
status		
statistic	statistician, statistical, statistically	
stress	stressful, stressfully, stressed	

Base word	Common forms	Translation/model sentence
structure	structure, structuralism, structural, structurally, structured	
style	stylist, style (v), stylish, stylistic, stylised	
summarize	summary, summation, summarily	
survivor	survival, survivalist, survive, surviving	
suspend	suspension, suspended	
sustainability	sustain, sustainable, sustained	
symbol	symbolism, symbolize, symbolic, symbolically	
target	target (v), targeted	
technique		
theory	theorist, theorize, theoretical, theoretically	
topic	topicality, topical	
tradition	traditionalist, traditional, traditionally	
transfer	transferability, transference, transferable	
transport	transport, transporter, transport (v)	
trend	trendy	
unique	uniqueness, uniquely	
variation	vary, varied	
vehicle	vehicular	
version		
virtual	virtually	
visual	vision, visualize, visually	
volunteer	volunteer (v), voluntary, voluntarily	
whereas		

Introduction

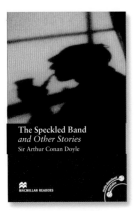

The Dancing Men is taken from *The Speckled Band and Other Stories* by Arthur Conan Doyle, a title from the Macmillan Readers series.

About the author

Sir Arthur Conan Doyle was born on 22 May 1859, in Edinburgh, Scotland. At the age of nine, his parents sent him away to a strict boarding school in England, where he stayed until the age of seventeen. Those adolescent years were difficult and lonely ones, but it was during that time that Conan Doyle discovered a talent for writing.

After graduating from Edinburgh University in 1876, Conan Doyle served as a ship's doctor on the African coast before returning home and setting up a medical practice in Plymouth. However, the practice didn't do very well, and he filled the time in between seeing his small number of patients with writing stories. As a result, he published his first Sherlock Holmes novel, *A Study in Scarlet*, in 1888.

Conan Doyle went on to publish many more stories about the clever detective and the stories became very popular. But Conan Doyle eventually became tired of Holmes. He wanted to concentrate on other, more serious writing, so he tried to kill the detective by making him fall over a waterfall in the story *The Final Problem*. The public, however, were furious about the death of their favourite detective and demanded that Conan Doyle brought the character back to life! Later, he did exactly that in the story *The Adventure of the Empty House*.

Conan Doyle also published science fiction, historical novels, romances, and non-fiction, including *The Great Boer War* in 1900, which described the time he spent working as a doctor in the South African War of 1899–1902. The book supported England's reasons for entering the war, and Conan Doyle believed that this was why he received a knighthood on his return to England.

During his later years, Conan Doyle developed an interest in Spiritualism, declaring a belief in the existence of fairies and other mythical creatures. He wrote several books about this subject, including *The Coming of the Fairies* in 1922. Sir Arthur Conan Doyle died of a heart attack on 7 July 1930. He was seventy-one years old.

The Dancing Men

1 *A Strange Drawing*

One morning, Sherlock Holmes handed me a sheet of paper.

'Look, Watson,' he said. 'Can you explain this problem?'

I looked at the paper. To my surprise, it was covered with a line of strange pictures. These pictures looked like little dancing men.

'A child must have drawn these,' I said. 'Where did you get this piece of paper, Holmes?'

'It arrived by post this morning,' answered Holmes. 'A man called Hilton Cubitt, of Ridling Thorpe Manor in Norfolk, sent it to me. Mr Cubitt is coming to see me today.

'There's a ring at the doorbell, Watson. Perhaps that's Mr Cubitt now.'

A moment later, a tall gentleman entered the room. He had a handsome face with clear blue eyes and looked very strong, and healthy.

This gentleman shook hands with both of us. Suddenly he caught sight of the strange drawings.

'Here's a mystery, Mr Holmes,' he said. 'What do you think of these drawings?'

'They look like children's drawings,' replied Holmes. 'But why do you think they are important?'

'I don't, Mr Holmes. But these drawings are making my wife very frightened. That's why I have come to see you. I want to find out what they mean.'

Holmes held up the paper, so that the sunlight shone through it. It was a page torn from a notebook and the markings on it looked like this:

Holmes examined the paper carefully. Then he folded it up and put it in his pocket.

'This is a most interesting and unusual case, Mr Cubitt,' he said. 'Please tell us your story from the beginning.'

2 *Mr Cubitt's Story*

'I'm not very good at telling stories,' said Mr Cubitt. 'But first, I want to explain something.

'I'm not rich, but I come from a very old and well-known family. My family has lived at Ridling Thorpe Manor, in Norfolk, for nearly five hundred years.

'Last year, while I was visiting London, I met an American lady called Elsie Patrick. Elsie and I became friends and soon fell in love. I didn't know anything about Elsie's family or her past life. But I decided to ask her to marry me.

'The day before our wedding, Elsie spoke to me. 'I've had some very sad things happen to me in my past life, Hilton. I've done nothing wrong, but I wish to forget my past. Please promise me you will never ask me anything about it. If you are unable to make this promise, then please go back to Norfolk and leave me.'

'So I promised Elsie I would never ask her anything about her past life. We've been married for a year now and we've been very happy. During all this time, I've kept my promise. But one day, about a month ago, my wife received a letter from America – I saw the American stamp. She read the letter and her face turned white. Then she threw the letter in the fire.

'She said nothing, but from that time, there's been a look of fear on her face.

'Mr Holmes, my wife is a very good woman. I'm sure she has not done anything wrong in her past life.

'But Elsie knows I am very proud of my family. My family's long history is very important to me. She would never do anything to upset me. Perhaps that's the reason she's afraid to tell me her troubles.'

'Please go on,' said Holmes.

'Well,' continued Mr Cubitt, 'yesterday morning, a strange thing happened. I found this piece of paper lying on the sundial in the garden. At first, I thought it was a child's drawing.

'But when I showed the paper to Elsie, she fainted. Since then, she has seemed like someone in a dream, and there is terror in her eyes.

'I didn't know what to do. If I took the paper to the police, they would laugh at me. So I came to you. Mr Holmes, please help me. I'm not rich, but I'll spend all my money to protect my wife from danger.'

I was sorry for Mr Cubitt. He was a good man and I saw that he loved his wife very much.

Holmes did not speak for some time.

'Mr Cubitt, don't you think,' he said at last, 'you should ask your wife to tell you everything?'

'I found this piece of paper lying on the sundial.'

'But I promised Elsie I would never ask her about her past,' replied Hilton Cubitt. 'If she wants to tell me something, she will. But I will not ask her to tell me.'

'I'll be pleased to help you,' said Holmes. 'I believe there is a meaning in the pictures of the dancing men. But I need more information before I can say what it is.

'Go back to Norfolk. If there are any more pictures of dancing men, make a copy of them for me. If anything important happens, I'll come to Norfolk at once.'

3 *Mr Cubitt's Second Visit*

During the next few days, Holmes was very quiet. Several times he looked at the paper with the dancing figures on it.

Then one afternoon, about a fortnight later, we had another visit from Mr Cubitt. He seemed worried and tired.

'My wife hasn't told me anything yet, Mr Holmes,' he said. 'But I have more pictures of dancing men and – more important – I've seen the man who draws them.

'But I'll tell you everything that has happened. The morning after I visited you, I found another line of dancing men. They were drawn with chalk on the toolhouse which stands in the garden, near the house. I made this copy.'

Hilton Cubitt unfolded a paper and laid it on the table.

'Excellent!' cried Holmes. 'Please go on.'

'After I'd made the copy,' continued Mr Cubitt, 'I cleaned off the marks. But two days later, another drawing appeared. Here it is:

Holmes was delighted.

'We're beginning to get a lot of information,' he said.

'I decided to find out who was drawing these pictures,' went on Hilton Cubitt. 'So the next night, I took my gun and sat beside a window which looks out onto the garden.

'At about two o'clock in the morning, my wife came into the room. She was wearing her night clothes. She asked me to come to bed. But I refused.

"No, Elsie,' I said. 'I want to see who is drawing these pictures.'

'Suddenly I saw Elsie's face turn very white in the moonlight. She was looking out of the window. I looked out of the window, too. I saw something moving near the toolhouse. A dark figure came slowly round the corner of the toolhouse and stopped beside the door.

'Immediately, I picked up my gun. I wanted to run out of the house, but my wife caught me in her arms and held me back. By the time I got outside, the man was gone.

'On the toolhouse door was the same drawing I copied before:

'I looked everywhere, but I couldn't find the man. However, in the morning, when I looked at the toolhouse door again, I saw a second line of dancing men. This new line is very short, but I made a copy and here it is.'

Hilton Cubitt gave another piece of paper to Holmes.

I could see that Holmes was very excited.

'Tell me,' he said, 'was this second line of figures separate from the first?'

'It was on a different part of the door.'

'Excellent!' cried Holmes. 'This last drawing is very important. It makes me feel hopeful. Please continue your interesting story.'

'I've nothing more to say,' replied Hilton Cubitt, 'except, I was angry with Elsie for holding me back. I'm sure she knows who this man is and what these pictures mean.

'Now I must go back to Norfolk. Elsie is very frightened and I don't want to leave her alone at night.'

'Well,' said Holmes, 'please leave these pictures with me. I will examine them carefully. I think I'll be able to solve the mystery soon.'

'A dark figure came slowly round the corner of the toolhouse and stopped beside the door.'

4   *Terrible News*

As soon as Hilton Cubitt left the room, Holmes ran to a table. He put all the papers with pictures of dancing men on the table. He began to examine them carefully.

For the next two hours, Holmes worked hard examining the papers. At last, he jumped up excitedly. Then he sat down again and wrote out a long telegram.

'As soon as we get an answer to this telegram, Watson,' he said, 'we'll visit Mr Cubitt in Norfolk. I have some important information for him.'

I was very curious about the telegram. I very much wanted to know what Holmes had found out about the meaning of the dancing men. But I didn't ask any questions. I knew Holmes would tell me when he was ready.

Two days passed. Then on the evening of the second day, Holmes received another letter from Hilton Cubitt.

In this letter, Mr Cubitt said he had found a new drawing of dancing men. He had found the drawing that morning, on the sundial in the garden. Mr Cubitt had made a copy of the drawing in his letter:

Holmes examined these pictures carefully. Suddenly he jumped up.

'We must go to Norfolk at once, Watson,' he said.

At that moment, a telegram arrived for Holmes. It was the answer he had been waiting for. Holmes read the telegram and his face looked serious.

'Mr Cubitt is in terrible danger,' he said. 'He needs our help.'

But, unfortunately, we were not able to go to Norfolk that evening. It was late and the last train had gone. The next train was not until the morning. In the morning, we travelled to Norfolk. At the station, we asked our way to Ridling Thorpe Manor.

'Are you the detectives from London?' the stationmaster asked.

'Why do you think we are detectives from London?' asked Holmes in surprise.

'Because the Norfolk police are already on their way to Ridling Thorpe Manor,' said the stationmaster. 'But perhaps you are doctors? The lady isn't dead yet. You may be in time to save her life.'

Holmes looked very worried.

'What do you mean?' he asked. 'What has happened at Ridling Thorpe Manor?'

'It's terrible news,' replied the stationmaster. 'Both Mr Hilton Cubitt and his wife have been shot. Mr Cubitt is dead and his wife is seriously injured.'

5   *The Investigation Begins*

At once, Holmes hurried to a carriage. During the journey to Ridling Thorpe Manor, he did not speak at all. But I could see he was very worried.

Holmes had known that Hilton Cubitt was in danger. But he had not arrived in time to save his client.

At last, we could see a large, old house through the trees. This was Ridling Thorpe Manor. As we came near the front door, I saw the toolhouse and the sundial in the garden. These were the places where Hilton Cubitt had found pictures of dancing men.

A carriage was standing outside the front door and a small man was getting out. This man introduced himself as Inspector Martin of the Norfolk police. Holmes introduced himself to Inspector Martin.

Inspector Martin was very surprised when he heard my friend's name.

'But, Mr Holmes,' he said, 'the crime was committed only a few hours ago, at three o'clock this morning! How did you get here from London so quickly?'

'When I left London, I didn't know a crime had been committed,' replied Holmes. 'I was on my way here to prevent a crime. But I've arrived too late.

'Now, Inspector Martin, shall we work together on this investigation? Or do you want to work alone?'

'I'd be very pleased to work with you,' replied the inspector.

'Good,' said Holmes. 'Then let's try to find out what happened.'

At that moment, the doctor, an old, white-haired man, came downstairs from Mrs Cubitt's room. The doctor said the lady was very badly injured, but that she would not die.

The bullet which wounded Mrs Cubitt had gone into her brain. The gun which fired the bullet had been very close to her. Hilton Cubitt had been shot through the heart.

A gun had been found lying halfway between the two bodies. Two shots had been fired from the gun.

But we did not know if Mrs Cubitt had shot her husband first, and then shot herself. Or if Mr Cubitt had shot his wife, and then killed himself.

'Has Mr Cubitt's body been moved?' asked Holmes.

'No,' replied the doctor. 'We had to move the lady. We couldn't leave her lying injured on the floor.'

'Who found the body?'

'Two of the servants,' said the doctor.

'Then let's hear their story,' said Holmes.

The two women told their story very clearly. They had been awakened from their sleep by a loud noise. A minute later, they heard another noise.

Both women ran downstairs from their rooms. The door of a downstairs room was open and Mr Cubitt lay dead on the floor.

Near the window, his wife was sitting with her head against the wall. One side of her face was red with blood.

The window was shut and the room was full of smoke and the smell of gunpowder.

Immediately, the two servants sent for the doctor. When he arrived, they carried Mrs Cubitt upstairs.

The servants did not understand why the crime had been committed. Mr and Mrs Cubitt had been in love with each other and had never quarrelled.

'Tell me,' said Holmes, 'when did you first notice the smell of gunpowder?'

'When we ran out of our rooms upstairs,' replied the women.

'Good,' said Holmes. 'Now let's examine the room downstairs.'

Mr Cubitt lay dead on the floor. His wife was sitting with her head against the wall.

6 *Holmes Sends a Note*

The room was small, with a window looking onto the garden. Mr Cubitt's body lay on the floor.

'You can take away the body now,' said Holmes. Then he turned to the doctor. 'Have you found the bullet which injured Mrs Cubitt?' he asked.

'No,' replied the doctor. 'The bullet is still somewhere in her brain. We will have to operate to remove the bullet.'

'We know that two bullets were fired from the gun,' said Inspector Martin. 'And we know where each bullet went. One bullet killed Mr Cubitt and the other injured his wife.'

'Yes,' said Holmes, 'but what about the third bullet – the bullet which passed through the window frame?'

He turned suddenly and pointed to a hole in the bottom of the window frame. This hole was the exact shape and size of a bullet.

'Wonderful!' cried Inspector Martin. 'Then three shots were fired, not two. A third person was in the room.

'But, Mr Holmes, how did you know a bullet had passed through the window frame?'

'Well,' said Holmes, 'you remember that the two servants smelt gunpowder as soon as they left their rooms?'

'Yes,' said the inspector, 'but I still don't understand.'

'The servants' rooms are upstairs. But the gun was fired downstairs. So the smell of the gunpowder must have been blown from this room to the rooms upstairs. Therefore the window must have been open.

'A third person could have stood outside the window and fired through it. If somebody inside the room fired at this person and missed, the bullet would pass through the window frame.'

'I understand,' said Inspector Martin. 'But when the servants entered this room, they said the window was shut.'

'That was because Mrs Cubitt had just shut it,' replied Holmes. 'But what's this?'

A lady's handbag was standing on a small table. I saw it was full of money. The money was tied together. We counted twenty fifty-pound notes.

'This money is important evidence,' said Holmes. 'And now let's find out where the third bullet went, after it passed through the window frame.'

We all went outside into the garden. There were flowers planted underneath the window. The flowers were broken and there were large footprints on the ground.

Holmes searched in the grass. Suddenly he bent forward and picked something up. It was the missing bullet.

'I think, Inspector,' he said, 'that our case is nearly solved.'

'But, Mr Holmes,' said the inspector, 'who was this other person and how did he get away?'

'I will tell you later,' said Holmes. 'First, I want to know if there is a place near here called Elrige's?'

We asked the servants, but none of them had ever heard the name. Then the boy who worked with the horses remembered a farm with that name. This farm was a very lonely place, many miles away, near a village called East Rushton.

Holmes thought for a moment, then he smiled strangely.

'Bring a horse,' he said to the boy. 'I want you to take a message to Elrige's Farm.'

Then Holmes took from his pocket all the papers with the pictures of the dancing men on them. He sat down at a table and worked carefully. Finally, he handed a note to the boy.

'Give this note to the person whose name is written on the outside,' said Holmes. 'And don't answer any questions.'

I looked at the outside of the note. It was addressed, in large writing, to: *Mr Abe Slaney, Elrige's Farm, East Rushton, Norfolk.*

Then Holmes turned to Inspector Martin.

'I think you should get more policemen,' he said. 'We'll have to catch a dangerous criminal.'

7   *Holmes Explains the Mystery*

After the boy had left, Holmes gave some instructions to the servants.

'If anybody comes and asks for Mrs Cubitt,' he said, 'do not tell the person that she is ill. Show the person straight into the sitting-room.

'There are some things I want to explain,' Holmes said. Then he told the inspector about Hilton Cubitt's visits to us in London and the pictures of the dancing men.

'These drawings are a kind of secret writing,' said Holmes. 'They look like children's drawings, but they are messages. Each picture of a dancing man is a letter of the alphabet. Let me show you how it works.

'The letter of the alphabet which appears most often in English is 'E.' The picture of the dancing man which appeared most often

was ⵎ So I knew that this picture was 'E.'

'Some of the dancing men were holding flags. I guessed that a figure with a flag was the last letter of a word.'

'But how did you find out what the other pictures meant?' I asked.

'On Hilton Cubitt's second visit,' went on Holmes, 'he brought three different messages with him. The last message was:

'In this message, there was no flag. So the message had to be one, single word. What could it be?

'The word had five letters, and the second and fourth letters were 'E.' It might be 'SEVER' or 'LEVER' or 'NEVER.' But the most probable of these words was 'NEVER.' So I knew the

pictures  were 'N,' 'V' and 'R.' '

'Excellent, Holmes!' I cried. 'What did you do next?'

'Well,' said Holmes, 'I knew Mrs Cubitt's first name was Elsie. I noticed that there was another word which had five letters and began and ended with 'E.'

'So I guessed that and were probably 'L,' 'S' and 'I.'

'In one message, the word 'ELSIE' was written twice. In this message, the word before 'ELSIE' had four letters and ended with 'E.' I guessed the writer was asking Elsie to do something.

'So now I looked for an English word of four letters ending in 'E.' The best word I could think of was 'COME.'

'So now I knew that and were 'C,' 'O' and 'M.'

'Then I looked again at the first message which Hilton Cubitt brought us:

'I used the figures holding flags to divide the message into words. I wrote out the message, putting dots for the letters I didn't know.

.M .ERE . .E SL .NE .

'The first missing letter had to be 'A' and the second letter had to be 'H.'

AM HERE A .E SLANE .

'Clearly, the two missing letters were part of somebody's name. So it must be:

AM HERE ABE SLANEY

'Then I looked at the second message again:

'This message worked out like this:

A . ELRI . ES

'Here, I worked out that the missing letters could be 'T' and 'G.'

AT ELRIGES

'I decided to find out if there was a place near Ridling Thorpe Manor that was called Elrige's. If there was, then I knew that this was where the writer of the messages was staying.'

Inspector Martin and I looked at Holmes. It was wonderful how my friend had found out the meaning of the dancing men.

'What did you do then, Mr Holmes?' asked the inspector.

'I guessed that Abe Slaney was an American. 'Abe' is an American name and Mrs Cubitt had recently received a letter from America. This letter had upset her very much.

'So I sent a telegram to a friend in the New York Police, asking about Abe Slaney. This was the reply:

THE MOST DANGEROUS CROOK IN CHICAGO

'The same evening, I received Hilton Cubitt's final message. The message worked out like this:

ELSIE . RE . ARE TO MEET THY GO .

Clearly, the missing letters had to be 'P' and 'D.'

ELSIE PREPARE TO MEET THY GOD

'I knew the Cubitts were in terrible danger. Abe Slaney was saying he was going to kill Mrs Cubitt. So Dr Watson and I hurried immediately to Norfolk, but, unfortunately, we were too late. Hilton Cubitt was dead.'

'But what about Abe Slaney, Mr Holmes?' asked Inspector Martin. 'If he is the murderer and he's at Elrige's, he may escape.'

'Don't worry,' said Holmes. 'He won't escape. He's coming here.'

'Here?' said Inspector Martin, in surprise. 'Why should he come here?'

'Because I have written and asked him to come here.'

Holmes stood up and walked to the window. 'Look, here he is!'

8 *The Murderer is Caught*

A man was coming up the path. He was tall and handsome, with a large, black beard. The front doorbell rang loudly.

'Hide behind the door,' said Holmes quietly. 'This man is very dangerous and we must be careful.'

We waited in silence for a minute. Then the sitting-room door opened and the man stepped into the room. At once, Holmes put a gun against his head and Inspector Martin put handcuffs on his wrists.

The man looked at us. His black eyes looked angry.

'I received a note from Mrs Cubitt,' he said. 'Where is she?'

'Mrs Cubitt is badly injured,' replied Holmes. 'Her life is in great danger.'

The man cried out. He sat down on a chair and put his face in his hands.

'I didn't know she was injured,' he said. 'I shot her husband when he tried to kill me. But I would never injure Elsie. I love her more than anything in the world.'

Suddenly, the man looked up.

'Wait,' he said. 'If Elsie is badly injured, who wrote this?'

He opened his hands and threw a note onto the table.

'I wrote it, to make you come here,' said Holmes.

'You wrote it? But how could you know the meaning of the dancing men?'

'I worked out what the figures meant,' replied Holmes. 'But now, tell us your story.'

'All right,' said the man. 'If Elsie dies, it doesn't matter what happens to me.

'My name is Abe Slaney and I've known Elsie since she was a child. Her father was head of a gang of crooks in Chicago and I was a member of the gang.

'Elsie's father thought of the secret writing of the dancing men. The members of the gang used it to send messages to one another.

'Elsie and I were engaged to be married. But Elsie hated her father's business and she didn't want to be married to a criminal. So she ran away to England. She met and married this Englishman, Hilton Cubitt.

'I wrote to Elsie, but she didn't answer my letters. In the end, I came to England and stayed at Elrige's Farm.

'I knew Elsie understood the pictures of the dancing men. So I left messages where she would see them. In the messages, I asked her to come away with me. But her only answer was 'Never.'

'Then Elsie wrote me a letter. She said she would meet me at three o'clock in the morning, when her husband was asleep.

'She brought money with her. She offered me the money and asked me to go away. I became angry and tried to pull her through the window.

'Just then, her husband rushed in, carrying a gun. He fired the gun at me and missed. At the same moment, I shot at him and he fell down dead.

'I ran across the garden. As I ran, I heard the window shut behind me.

'I have told you the truth, gentlemen. I didn't know Elsie was hurt. She must have shot herself after I left.'

While Abe Slaney was talking, a carriage arrived with two policemen in it. Inspector Martin turned to his prisoner.

'It's time for us to go, Slaney. Goodbye, Mr Holmes. I hope I'll work with you again one day.'

As the carriage drove away, I saw the note which Abe Slaney had thrown on the table. This was what Holmes had written:

'If you work it out, Watson,' said Holmes, 'you'll find it means: 'Come here at once.'

'I knew Abe Slaney would come when he read the note. He would think Mrs Cubitt had written it.'

'Well,' I said, 'criminals have used the dancing men to help them in their crimes. But now the dancing men have been used to catch a criminal.'

'Yes,' said Holmes. 'The dancing men have finally done some good.'

At once, Holmes put a gun against his head and Inspector Martin put handcuffs on his wrists.